Copyright C

Edited by Christopher Moore, Must Kill Chris Books

All rights reserved. No part of this book may be reproduced in any form or by any means, except by inclusion of brief quotations in a review, without permission in writing from the publisher. The author retains copyright of his own individual story.

This book is a not work of fiction. The situations in this book are not imaginary but names and place names may have been tampered with. All resemblances are accurate of all characters, living or dead.

This book is sold subject to the condition that it shall not, by way of trade or otherwise, be lent, resold, hired out or otherwise circulated without the publisher's prior consent in any form or binding or cover other than that in which it is published and without similar condition including this condition being imposed on the subsequent purchaser

Published in Great Britain in 2020 by Christopher Moore

Must Kill Chris Books, Somewhere in Suffolk, UK

Christopher Moore

In Amongst the Peacocks
Christopher Moore

Christopher Moore

Au Revoir

When I was a child I was an extremely good boy. I was always helpful, very polite and never any trouble at all. At least that's what I like to tell my daughter Faith whenever she asks me about my childhood, however, if I'm honest that wasn't always strictly the case. While it's true in some respects I was a very good child, my bedroom for instance was always spotless, in other respects I'm sure I was a challenge as a son. I know I've certainly kept my parents on their toes growing up and even now, as a forty-year-old adult, I probably still cause more than my fair share of headaches in their lives. Even though I've gotten older and accomplished all the normal things you would expect of a man my age, like getting married and having children, I've never really grown up. In fact, I'm not convinced anyone ever really does.

When you're young you look up to adults, especially your parents, and see them as mature and responsible people. If there's a crisis, they're the ones who'll sort it. If you have a question, they'll have the answer. They are a stable constant while you grow, learn and make all the mistakes you're supposed to make on the way to adulthood. The problem with this image they present is that it's nothing more than smoke and mirrors, the illusion of security. The majority of adults have no better idea what they're doing or where they're going than their bewildered offspring. So it came as something of a surprise to me when I reached adulthood and realised that I wouldn't magically become this responsible pillar of the community, in fact, truth be told, when I became an adult I probably made more mistakes than I did as a child. When you're older you're still the same person you were when you were younger, the only difference is, if you break something, you pay for it.

This book is my autobiography, sort of.

I'm not a famous person, not even locally, outside of my relatively small circle of family and friends, nobody would know who I am. Likewise, I'm not a master of social media either, my Facebook friends currently number less than forty and my Instagram account, while well used, is kept set to private. With these things in mind it stands to reason that not many people would be interested in the details of my life at all. I'm sure my day to day existence is pretty typical of an ordinary person but, like any other ordinary person, in my life things often don't turn out the way I plan them to. I think if most people were to sit down and tell you their life story, they'd probably want to make sure you heard the good bits, their triumphs, their achievements, how they made their fortune and how nice the view is from their villa in Spain. I don't have a long list of achievements and accolades to drone on about for hours on end, what I do have is a real life that's full of all the bits other people might decide to omit from their stories. I am of course referring to the embarrassments, the humiliations, the failures and the times when I took the low road. The dirt. That's the fun stuff, right? Because the truth is, we all have these sorts of stories, I've just written mine down.

I was born in April 1979, at Ipswich hospital in Suffolk, to my parents George and Jane. I lived in East Bergholt until I was about seven before moving with my parents and two younger sisters, Caroline and Kristy, to a house in the nearby village of Brantham, which is about twenty minutes' drive from Ipswich and the house my parents still live in to this day.

My childhood was a happy one for the most part; my parents were, and are, fantastic people and did everything they could for myself and my sisters, I only say "for the most part" because high school was not the best experience for me and I struggled for a while with bullies. A bully's actions reflect much more on themselves than they do on the victim of their abuse, they don't exist in my story and will receive no further mention from me for the duration of the book. If you are the victim of a bully just remember, whether the bully is male or female, they're doing it because they have a very small penis.

My favourite time, as a child, was always Christmas. My parents always went to a lot of trouble to make sure that it was a magical time of year for both myself and my sisters. This was something I never forgot and that I tried to continue for my own children, Christina and Faith, although I don't think I ever succeeded in the way my parents did. I can picture the house in my head now, immaculately decorated with the smell of pine in the air emanating from a perfectly decorated, real Christmas tree. The anticipation for Christmas Day was almost unbearable, we'd never get to see a present in the house before we woke up Christmas morning so sleeping Christmas Eve was next to impossible. Every year we woke our parents up at first light, actually in winter first light is about seven so let me try again... Every year we woke our parents up several hours before first light without fail and we'd sit at the top of the stairs waiting for permission to race down to see what had appeared while we slept, that time sat at the top of the stairs, ready to get my Christmas on, is my favourite memory from those days.

One Christmas I remember my dad gave me a WWE themed duvet set for my bed. It featured Hulk Hogan, Macho Man Randy Savage and The Ultimate Warrior on both duvet and pillow, flexing their larger than life oily muscles. I've always been a huge fan of wrestling, and I still am, but I must say that at eighteen years of age this gift, obviously aimed at much younger children, was quite a shock. As I tore off the wrapping paper and looked inside I wondered, if I was able to somehow to convince a girl to come home with me, how I would then convince her to stay with Hulkamania running wild all over my sheets? I obviously didn't mask this worry very well because my father instantly picked up on my distress and offered to return the gift, I hoped I hadn't hurt his feelings but I felt relieved that I didn't have to sleep with those three wrestlers.

Despite that rare slip up, my parents always gave us an amazing Christmas and I'm very grateful for all the work they put in to make sure my childhood was full of happy memories.

I went to school at Brookside Primary followed by Eastwood High School, class of 95. When I left I went on to college where I studied art and then later graphic design. During college I worked for an agency temping in various factories but my first real job came after I left college, when I worked for a supermarket as a bakery assistant. I stayed there for several years until I landed a job as a graphic designer working for a company called Pilkington Design & Print, before eventually managing their large format print division.

In 2014 I suffered a nervous breakdown due to the stresses involved in my working life and I was left unable to work. Since that time I have concentrated on creative pursuits to both keep my mind occupied and work towards recovery. In 2015 I released an album called *The Bearded Man* under the name Must Kill Chris which received very positive reviews and some airplay on BBC radio. I've worked with the band Love Zombies; I had the privilege of designing the artwork for their debut album *Passionfruit* and had a fantastic experience recording with them at Abbey Road Studios on their second album *No Slow Songs*. I also had my first short story published in a horror anthology put together by Matthew Cash of Burdizzo Books.

As a result of my mental illness I lost a lot, including my wife, my home and, worst of all, the freedom to see my daughters every day. I started again from nothing at thirty-five years old, having to rebuild my life from the ground up. I like to think that, as well as being a good father to my daughters, the ability to be creative and work on these projects gives my life some small value and the strength to carry on in the face of this illness.

Although the stories contained within this book are one hundred percent true, the names of some of the people, locations and corporations have been changed to protect their identities... and to prevent them from suing my arse.

The Peacock & the Doctor

This is probably the earliest memory I have so for me this has to be where my story begins. I would have been about five years old at the time which would make the year 1984.

As I was quite young I don't remember too much about those days, just the highlights of growing up in the eighties which in all fairness was probably one of the best times it was possible to grow up. There was a sense of fun and freedom that seems to be lost in childhood these days with children glued to their smart phones and televisions happy to stay in front of the warm glow of a screen instead of being outside in the sunshine. I remember being able to leave the house in the morning, get on my BMX and just disappear with my friends for the whole day. We didn't have mobile phones, nobody cared where we went or what we did there was just one rule which was 'be home for tea'. As long as you reappeared by the time dinner was on the table nobody batted an eyelid. I'll always remember my childhood up until high school as one of the best times in my life.

It's impossible for me to talk about the eighties without at least mentioning the music. By the time I was old enough to take a serious interest in music it was the nineties and I was listening to bands like The Wildhearts, Nirvana and Green Day but long before that songs like 'Centerfold' by the J.Geils Band and 'Goody Two Shoes' by Adam Ant were laying the groundwork for my musical education. I had enjoyed eighties music as a child but it probably took another fifteen years or so before I began to look back with nostalgic eyes and appreciate just how good the music was that decade. If I'm feeling down in the dumps today I know that if I put an eighties playlist on and turn up the volume it will go a long way to lifting my spirits.

Still not everything in the Eighties was that great. I think if you were to look back at any pictures of me from that time you would definitely have been hard pressed not to laugh at my hair. I know it was the eighties, we all had bad hair and ridiculous clothes but my hair was worse than most because my dad had decided with, as far as I'm aware no previous barber training, that he could cut my hair for me. It was true I was a fidgety child and would not sit still for any barber they tried to take me to so I probably brought it all on myself but that does nothing to make me feel better when confronted with the pictures. The two unavoidable facts of the matter were:

1. My dad cut my hair and...

2. My mum used to cry when he was finished.

I have two stories from when I was this age that both take place in a zoo. The first I don't really remember so I can't talk about it with any great detail other than what my parents have told me. According to their account, I was off on my own feeding the monkeys a short distance away from where they were seated when I accidentally dropped the bag of monkey food on the floor spilling the contents. This obviously caused me some distress, I was so upset I ran back to my parents screaming as loud as my little lungs would allow "Mummy, Mummy, I dropped my nuts!" much to the amusement of both my parents and the other families attending the zoo that day. The other incident I remember much better indeed, probably because it was quite a lot worse than the events I've just described.

It all started pleasantly enough. My father had driven us to Banham Zoo in Norfolk for a family day out. I loved animals and I was very excited to be going. When we arrived at the zoo we made our way around the various attractions until eventually we came across a patch of open grass with gravel pathways where I spotted a group of peacocks strutting around. Naturally being only five years old and intrigued by not only the brightly coloured feathers but also by the fact they weren't in an enclosure, I wanted to grasp the opportunity to catch a peacock. This of course would be easier said than done but my mind was made up instantaneously, I was giving chase. I took off across the grass as fast as my little legs would carry me ignoring my mum's cries of "Stop" and "Don't run". I didn't care. I had a peacock to catch. The Peacocks were surprisingly fast and if I'm honest I didn't have much of a shot of actually catching one. Maybe if I'd been stealthy about it, took my time and snuck up on them I'd have been able to get close at least but in hindsight running at them as fast as possible and shouting is probably not the ideal tactic for catching birds. As it turned out, whether or not I caught a peacock would soon be the least of my worries. Like a coyote chasing a roadrunner I was completely obsessed with catching my target, I gave zero attention to the transition between grass and gravel on the ground below me and for that I paid the price. All of a sudden my feet lost traction on the loose gravel and slid out from underneath me, I was going down. I hit the deck hard slicing open my right knee as I landed. I cried out in pain, tears already flooding my eyes as I looked around for my family. My parents rushed towards me somehow maintaining their footing on the perilous surface, I could see the looks of concern on their faces, they were worried, though obviously not worried enough to compromise their grip on the loose pebbles. When they finally reached me they were able to see the full extent of my injury, the cut was deep, without question too deep for a plaster and an ice cream to fix. I needed medical attention and I needed it urgently.

We left the zoo post haste, I was carried out to the car and as my parents set out to find the location of the nearest emergency doctor I silently cursed my feathered nemesis, that peacock had bested me this time but in that moment I was sure one day our paths would cross again.

Actually to this day our paths have, as far as I know, never crossed again and following a quick Google search of the lifespan of your average peacock it seems as though I may have left it a little late. You win again Mr. Peacock. You win again.

I'm not sure how much time had passed but eventually we made it to the doctor's surgery, I was going to need stitches and so the doctor set to work patching me up. The first step in this process, as you will no doubt expect, was the removal of the bottom half of my clothing. I was now laying on the bed completely naked from the waist down with the doctor and both my parents stood over me. I'm not sure at all why I had to be stripped bare from the waist down. To this day the question plays on my mind because the cut was on my knee and I was wearing shorts... It's probably best not to think too hard about it. It's fine. It was probably fine. Medical reasons.

"Mum," I cried in a rather pathetic tone of voice, "I need the toilet." My bladder was full to the brim and as I was unable to remember when I last had opportunity to empty it. I felt it to be of the utmost importance that I be allowed to relieve myself as soon as possible.

"Shush", my mother replied, "you'll have to wait." I didn't get the impression she fully understood the gravity of my predicament and I felt compelled to plead my case as strongly as I knew how.

"I really need to go for a pee." I protested, "Please." I'm sure the desperation in my voice was more than adequate to convey my distress and I should have been rushed to a bathroom without delay.

Most people have been in a situation where they've been caught short and needed to find a toilet in an emergency but if you're laid flat on a table whilst someone is sewing your leg back together you've got little chance of making it to one any time soon. Still, despite it falling on deaf ears, I continued to request a bathroom break in the hopes that someone would give in and help me achieve total expulsion. They didn't. Eventually it got to the point that I'd just about had enough of not being listened to and I decided, using all the wisdom I had accrued in my five years on the planet, that there was only one thing left I could do. The doctor, busy sewing my knee back together, currently had his head closer to my private area than to my feet. Big mistake doc, big mistake indeed, he was mid stitch when I gave up the battle of wills with my bladder. A ferocious stream of hot urine arced from the tip of my penis and collided with the doctors left cheek, nose and mouth. There was an awkward moment of confusion on the doctor's part where he did not react, no doubt unsure of what exactly was happening to him as he focused in earnest on the stitching together of flesh. I watched for a second as the warm droplets of pee rolled off freely from the doctor's bottom lip before he suddenly shot bolt upright and screamed in disgust giving me, the urinator, a small fright. I tried to maintain my composure as the doctor stared down angrily at the human fountain laying half naked in his office as I continued to go off like a sprinkler on a hot summer's day.

One of the clearest memories I have even now is of that of the doctor angrily storming out of his office dabbing at his face with a towel while my parents, looking absolutely mortified, were doing their best to offer their apologies. I lay there bathed happily in my own urine, relieved, safe in the knowledge that the worst of my ordeal was now surely over.

Since that fateful day I have been urinated on myself multiple times by both children and animals and I have never found it to be a pleasant experience. I have, however, never taken it full in the face from a stranger. I'll bet that poor doctor wishes he could say the same. I still have the scar on my knee to this day as a permanent reminder both not to run on gravel and to stay well away from little boys with no trousers, something which, to be fair, I undoubtedly would stay away from regardless. The doctor probably doesn't need a reminder.

Christopher Moore

Chocolate Fudge Ice Cream Sundae Supreme

Not absolutely everything in my life is toilet related although if you stopped reading after these first few stories you'd probably have to assume it was. In the first chapter I had a problem with a number one, in this second chapter, quite fittingly, it was a number two.

I was six years old and on route to the Shore Field Holiday Village in Bournemouth. When I was a child we often used to spend our holidays in Bournemouth in a caravan and it was one of my favourite times of year. I even enjoyed myself the year it rained every day without fail so all we could do was sit around the caravan watching television and the only thing the television in the caravan showed was *Robin Hood: Prince of Thieves* on a loop. To this day I don't think I've seen a single film more times than that one but I enjoyed it every time we watched it. "I'm going to cut your heart out with a spoon." - The Sheriff of Nottingham. Lovely stuff.

It was late May and the weather was pleasantly warm and sunny and, although there were strong gusts of wind from time to time, that didn't affect us while we were in the car and through the window of my father's sky blue Vauxhall Cavalier we enjoyed blue skies as we listened to Cliff Richard sing 'Summer Holiday' for what seemed like the hundredth time that journey. We always know we were going on holiday when we heard Cliff and his voice brought with it a sense of excitement for the week ahead. The other thing I enjoyed about our caravanning holidays was that our cousins usually came as well. My cousin Robert being only a few months younger than me was someone I spent a lot of time with growing up. It was always more fun to have a friend my own age to get in to trouble with while we were away plus when they played 'Superman' by Black Lace at the holiday disco I needed someone to slide across the dancefloor with when the song reached the "Superman" section. You can cover a surprising distance diving onto your belly in a Superman pose on a well varnished dance floor.

During our journey to the Shore Field Holiday Village we'd stopped at the services to break up the journey. There was a delightful picnic area where young families were gathered enjoying an ice cream in the sunshine before they returned to their travels. Whilst the adults took a rest from driving us kids were allowed to run around for a bit to burn off some energy before having some food to replenish said energy and then running around a little more. Soon enough though we were worn out and it was time to leave, there was still a fair bit of driving to do and the adults wanted to make it to the caravan park in good time. The only problem was that I was not ready to leave. I needed a poo.

The toilets at the services had not been well maintained so were not nice at all, "disgusting" was the word my father had used to describe them, in fact he had decided the toilets were so bad I was not allowed to use them to pass number twos full stop. This created quite the problem because if one cannot pass poops in the appropriate pooping receptacle where can one pass poops? As I mentioned earlier the surrounding area was full of families enjoying the day but my dad, after some scouting around, had found what he believed to be a location secluded enough for me to do my business without being seen by anyone. I looked around at the other children playing and wondered if they were allowed to use the toilet or if everyone had to use a bush because the toilets were that bad, I hoped my bush hadn't been soiled already by another child in need. I walked into the bush followed by my father who carried a toilet roll and a plastic bag. Even at six years of age and without carrying the story on any further this was not an experience I could leave with any shred of dignity. I hesitantly lowered my shorts as my father turned his back and, with a small push, I did what needed to be done. With my business concluded all that was left was the obligatory cleanup. It was simple enough you might think as all I had to do was wipe my posterior and place the dirty paper into the plastic bag my father held out, still with his back to me. A simple enough task certainly as long as there were no sudden gusts of wind everything would be absolutely hunky dory, unfortunately when you're trying to wipe your bottom in a picnic area without being spotted sometimes things just don't go to plan. I needed to keep my balance, I was very focused on that, the last thing I needed was to fall backwards into my steaming hot turd. Gingerly I held out the dirty paper poised to place it safely into the plastic bag but one strong gust of wind later and the excrement coated sheets were airborne flying over the green hills like kamikaze bombers looking for unsuspecting ships out at sea. Moments later a scream could be heard interrupting the serenity of the motorway services, something had happened, something bad.

I quickly pulled up my shorts, exited the bush and rejoined my family where we saw, just a short distance away, the source of the anguished cries. A young boy no older than I was at the time had been enjoying a lovely ice cream cone when, as he leant in for a lick, my dirty brown sheet had collided with the aforementioned ice cream cornet and stuck to the vanilla flavoured frozen treat. My family stood there dumbfounded, recoiling in horror at the scene before them unsure of what to do next. The parents of that child would certainly not be amused and would no doubt angrily search for the culprit. Without too much dawdling the adults quickly decided a hasty retreat to the car was probably a good idea. We peeled out of the car park like a getaway car in a bank robbery as my father put the holiday mix cassette back on the stereo and the soothing sound of 'Brown eyed girl' by Van Morrison filled the air.

The chances of a used piece of toilet roll landing in your ice cream cone as you eat it must be similar to the odds of getting hit by a bolt of lightning, in fact I would probably argue that it would be more likely to be hit by the lightning. That said I still wonder if that child grew up with an irrational fear of eating ice cream out in the open. I wonder if he could sit on the beach and calmly devour a ninety-nine with a flake or if he just couldn't trust the skies enough to ever truly enjoy the experience. Could it extend beyond the ice cream, what if he could no longer set foot outside his front door without glancing skyward. It's a sobering thought that the consequences of a seemingly inconsequential act like using a bush instead of a bathroom could affect someone else's life so dramatically.

Christopher Moore

Orange Christmas

My next story takes place a few years later when I was eight, I was quickly getting older… well aging two years since the previous chapter is faster than anyone would like. Still it's fun being eight or indeed any age where you're not considered completely responsible for your own actions. Your parents have the job of teaching you right from wrong so any mischief you find yourself in is merely a reflection of their parenting skills and not technically your own fault. It's also an age where the benefit of the doubt is still very much on your side, you can do a lot with the benefit of the doubt. As soon as get to an age where those advantages disappear so does a lot of the fun of being a kid.

It was Christmas 1987, my favourite time of year. It'd already been an exciting year because I always enjoyed a good storm and that October we experienced the Great Storm of 1987. Even at my young age I remember watching the weather on television with my parents when Michael Fish had opened his report with the words, "Good afternoon to you. Earlier on today, apparently a woman rang the BBC saying she heard that there was a hurricane on the way, well if you're watching, don't worry, there isn't." The very next day we were hit with hurricane-force winds of 122mph. I was in school the day of the storm and watched the events unfold from the safety of the classroom. My eyes were glued to the window as I hoped to see something fly past that shouldn't have been airborne, something along the lines of a car or a caravan would've been great but I'd have settled for a household pet, that would have been amazing. Although neither of those things occurred, I did get to see a tree or two get blown over which is still pretty exciting and certainly more than I've seen since.

In the run up to Christmas that year I'd been looking forward to attending the annual Christingle service at Brantham Church as we did every year. Church wasn't ever something I enjoyed apart from this one yearly occasion where they added in two things I enjoyed very much, namely food and playing with fire. If you didn't release an audible gasp at the idea of letting an eight-year-old boy loose with a naked flame as he sits with a group of other children also holding naked flames with limited adult supervision then you probably weren't paying close enough attention to the words as written. Feel free to loudly gasp now. Anyway, enough of this talk of flames and food, you're probably asking yourself at this point, hold on… what the hell is a bloody Christingle anyway? And you'd be right to ask because in the past whenever I've begun to tell this story to friends they've stared at me blankly as if the whole event was a figment of my imagination but it's not, it's flipping real and it happens every year on the first Sunday of Advent to celebrate Jesus Christ as the "light of the world".

I think, if anyone was wondering how to celebrate Jesus Christ as the "light of the world" I would probably assume we'd all come up with the same idea or a slight variation thereof so I'm not really sure of the need to explain further the exact nature of the Christingle. I will do so though just to cover all the bases. Firstly, you take an orange, your normal everyday orange you can find in any place that sells fruit, and you tie a red ribbon around it. Once the ribbon is tied then you need to add the candle. To do so, make a small hole at the top of the orange and force it inside, you may experience some loss of juice, I understand this is natural when something candle shaped is forced into an area too small to accommodate its presence, don't be concerned. Candle in place we skewer the area surrounding the candle with cocktail sticks and add onto those a range off sweets such as Jelly Tots or perhaps a selection of raisins and nuts. Once those sweets are added you have your finished Christingle, just add fire. I apologize for the long-winded explanation as, like I said before, I know in depicting Jesus Christ as the "light of the world" your mind naturally jumps to an orange and a candle.

I'm not sure the exact story of how the Christingle came to be but if I had to fill in the gaps in my knowledge without doing any real research I'd like to think this represents a pretty accurate picture of how it all went down.

A small congregation of vicars are sat around a long wooden table in all their religious garments as they wait impatiently for the last member of their order to arrive.

"Where's John?" asks the first vicar who is eager to get the meeting underway.

"Every single time he does this, he'll be at lunch." says another, "It's because we don't allow snacks during the meetings and he likes to make sure he's not going to be hungry while we're here."

Just then John enters the room, takes his chair within the group and the meeting commences, during which John nonchalantly pops on some shades, produces the Christingle from his vicar's robe with a flourish, lights the candle and starts plucking sweets from the ends of the cocktail sticks like a goddamn rockstar. The rest of the group turn and stare at John and another vicar bellows at him "For the last time John no snacking during the meeting. What on Earth is that thing anyway?"

John looks up innocently, "This thing? It's only a Christingle, the most religious snack there is. This snack represents Jesus Christ as the light of the world and we will use it to entice a new generation of followers into the church like a bunch of orangey pied pipers." With that he blows out the candle, removes his sunglasses and accepts the applause of his fellow vicars.

Like I said I'm not sure on the exact details but that'll be pretty damn close indeed.

Back then my family used to attend church on a Sunday because my mum enjoyed the peace and quiet there compared, I suppose, to putting up with me running around all over the place like a little Tasmanian Devil. While my parents attended church I was sent to Sunday school. I hated Sunday school, the idea itself made me angry. Even at that age I knew the weekend was invented to give children a break from school and now these religious types wanted to get me educated on a sixth day, I was having none of it. I made sure I wasn't there long; it was less than two months before they politely requested that I stopped attending due to my being a "disruptive influence". At eight years old I didn't really know what that meant but as I was rewarded with the return of my Sunday, I naturally assumed it was a good thing. The annual Christingle service was the only time I ever went willingly to church, their little ruse with the flaming snack had worked on me, I was hooked and I wanted that hot fruity treat all year long. It wasn't like a cheeky Easter egg either, you couldn't just go to the shop, get one a few months in advance and scoff it down without a second glance. Break out a Christingle outside of church and you're going to get looks.

This particular year when we attended the church it was packed to the rafters full of people all keen to celebrate how great Jesus was on the way to Christmas and our vicar had gone all out to impress the masses and deliver a kick arse sermon. My parents sat with the adults while I sat with the other Sunday school children, this was before my expulsion from Sunday school of course. After you've had your Christingle what's the point of going again until the following year anyway. For the purposes of illustrating the meaning of the different elements of the Christingle the vicar had gone to the trouble of creating a larger than life replica of this church-based treat which he introduced to us in sections explaining the meaning of each part of the Christingle as he went along. First the vicar held up a large papier mâché ball painted orange and asked the congregation what it was he was holding. After a few seconds somebody answered and told the vicar that it was in fact an orange, the delighted vicar knowing he was connecting with his flock went on to explain how this orange was symbolic of the world and that the red ribbon around it signifies the blood of Christ.

At this point the sermon couldn't have been going better. The vicar was confident. He'd put in the man-hours in preparation, he'd practiced for weeks on end in front of a mirror (probably) and the crowd were loving it. Inside his head I'm sure he would have been congratulating himself on a job well done.

For the next part of his explanation of the Christingle the vicar wanted to tell us about the candle, which represented Jesus' light in the world. This was arguably the most important part of the Christingle as it was, in effect, Jesus himself. The Vicar went back to his pulpit and produced his representation of a candle. Instantly I knew what this was. I was, after all, eight years old and I'd been around the block a time or two, this wasn't my first rodeo, I knew this was my time to shine. The vicar held his homemade replica candle aloft and asked his audience what it was he was holding. Without a second's hesitation and at the top of my voice I gave him his answer…

"It's a toilet roll!"

My words echoed through the church as a hushed silence fell over the congregation, except for the odd snigger of course. The vicar glared at me angrily as I looked back through the crowd at my parents disappointed faces. Maybe that was why I was removed from Sunday school, the vicar never forgave me, he didn't want me sullying his church by saying out loud what things actually were rather than what they represented. It wasn't very Christian of him I know but I'm sure I couldn't really have been so disruptive I was no longer welcome in the house of the lord so what other explanation could there be? Following my outburst, the other children thought I was the best thing since sliced Christingle, the vicar did not agree as his piece de resistance was ruined but I was just about as proud of myself as a little boy could be.

Christopher Moore

Dressed to Shepherd

Soon after the Christingle incident I was to be in Brookside Primary School's Christmas play. I wasn't comfortable with this at all, but when you're a child you're forced to take part in school plays at least once a year with no real way of avoiding them. Parents don't enjoy these plays any more than the children performing them and are forced onto impossibly uncomfortable wooden benches for several hours at a time constantly wondering if it would have really killed the school budget to splash out on a few cushions. I've always thought the school play was a scam invented by teachers to avoid doing any real educating in the run up to Christmas. As if teachers don't get enough time off.

I should say have seen all of my own daughter's school plays and I thoroughly enjoyed them all.

Times were different in the eighties and Brookside School was a miserable place, full of nasty teachers who got away with things they would never get away with these days and should never have gotten away with back then. On one occasion during a PE lesson I discovered, upon probing my mouth with my tongue, that I had a very slightly wobbly tooth. Our teacher, a mean-spirited old woman, stood at the front of the hall explaining the lesson to the class while I sat there listening quietly seeing how much movement there was in the aforementioned tooth with my thumb. The teacher noticed my slight distraction and sharply called my name ordering me to the front of the class where, not content with a stern telling off for playing with my tooth, she had me stand there in front of everyone and pull the tooth out of my mouth. The other children watched in horrified silence as I yanked and twisted the tooth trying as best I could to free it from the gum. It was not an easy task but I was not allowed to stop until it was completed. The hardest part for me, worse than the humiliation and worse than the pain was the sound, the sickening tearing sound that seemed to resonate inside my skull. After several minutes my tooth sprang free closely followed a large spurt of blood that made me choke and trickled down my chin. My teacher, looking very proud of herself for what she'd accomplished, then sent me to clean myself up before resuming the lesson. If the events I've just described were to happen today they would probably make the newspapers and the teacher in question would more than likely be suspended, investigated and then dismissed but back then it was just how things were.

That year's Christmas play was the classic story of the baby Jesus, well I'm pretty sure it was anyway, I was playing a shepherd and how many other plays can there be that feature shepherds? I was pleased that I didn't have a pivotal role in the play. Being in the background was enough for me as I didn't want to be there in the first place. Get in there, shepherd it up and get out again, that was the plan. It was down to the parents to supply our costumes for the play so I enlisted the help of my mother who, being my mother, was the woman I trusted most in the world to supply me with a costume that wouldn't make me look like a complete tit in front of the entire school. The finished article consisted

of a white tea towel wrapped around the head which was
held in place with red sweatband and a long robe type thing
made with an old white bedsheet which she had sewed
together. I was never going to look good wearing a tea towel
and a bedsheet but it was passable and passable was all I
needed. Nobody was going to be focusing on me anyway
being a lowly supporting cast member.

The day of the play arrived and I got into my costume
backstage, I say backstage I mean a classroom close to the
assembly hall where the play was taking place. I
haphazardly got myself ready, I was still unhappy about
being forced to take part when I noticed something that
would make me unhappier still, there was an issue with my
outfit. I could feel an unexpected breeze in my nether
regions, this concerned me because although a shepherd's
robes are pretty loose by design, they should still protect the
lower half from the elements. My mum had done her best
with my costume but unfortunately for me she was no
seamstress, the stitching holding the sheet together where it
covered my legs had come apart, and not just a little either
this was a huge wardrobe malfunction. I was now showing a
hell of a lot of leg. This was way too much leg for a
shepherd undoubtedly. I could say that there had never been
a shepherd showing off more leg than I was at that moment.
This could not happen. I was out. There was no way I was
going out there looking like I was trying to dress
provocatively for my shepherding duties, I wasn't trying to
pull a sheep for God's sake. As far as I was concerned the
play was off. I began to look around the classroom for an
escape route, an open window or perhaps at least a good spot

to hide when suddenly the door swung open and the evil
teacher who forced me to remove my tooth strode in like the
wicked witch in a fairy tale. The teacher saw what I was
wearing and laughed cruelly at was now, in effect, my dress.
I have never liked being laughed at and it put me on the
defensive.

"I'm not going out there," I insisted, "I look stupid.
There's no way you can make me." I folded my arms and
looked down at my skinny white legs in defiance.

My teacher's demeanor changed like the flicking of a
switch and she told me in no uncertain words that I was
going out there because if I refused, I would be letting
everybody down (I wouldn't), everyone was counting on me
(they weren't) and I had no choice (unfortunately that part
was correct). After going back and forth on it for some time
at some point I realised I wasn't going to win and I gave up
fighting. As the other three shepherds walked out from the
back of the assembly hall to the stage at the front they were
followed by a very reluctant, pissed off and yet somehow
sexier breed of shepherd.

I could hear the sniggers of the parents as I slowly
made my way past them all. Not only were all eyes on me,
which was the very thing I wanted to avoid, but now they
were all laughing too. I had never felt embarrassment on this
scale before, I was officially humiliated in front of everyone.
I put my head down and kept walking trying as best I as I
could to hold the sheet together to protect my modesty but it
was to no avail, I was exposed for the amusement of the
masses. After what seemed like an eternity, I made it to the

stage and I portrayed the role I'd been given to the utmost of my ability, which admittedly was not very well. Still I think even Tom Hanks would struggle if, as he tried to give a meaningful performance, he had to worry about his clothing falling apart while the rest of the production crew pointed and laughed. Jim Carrey on the other hand, is someone I think would nail it no matter what, but then, I'm no Jim Carrey. Eventually I finished my part in the play and I left the stage as fast as I possibly could. The ordeal was over.

After the weekend I returned to school. There'd be the odd snigger about the incident I was sure, the odd insult perhaps but before long it would all be forgotten. It wasn't until I arrived in our classroom that I saw it. They'd only taken photos; they'd only taken photos and made a flipping display on the wall. And what was the centrepiece? It was only me in my mother flipping dress.

The Ugly Stick

Even though I'd had my big moment of embarrassment in front of the class I was still a popular boy at primary school and had a fair few friends. When I reached approximately ten years old my best friends were twin brothers called Juice Steen and Stu Hart. I always liked the fact that nobody could tell the twins apart but me, which I found strange as Juice had a long face like a banana while Stu's was more squashed up and round like an orange. Surely anyone can tell the difference between a banana and an orange... apparently not. We used to get into all sorts of scrapes in the small village of Brantham where we all lived. In fact, there were some really random short stories that defy explanation during that time, they just sort of happened. The one that sticks in my head the most was when myself and the twins were riding our bikes near the field behind my house. A chubby blonde boy came around the corner and rode down the path towards us. We parked our bikes in front of him blocking the path as he approached forcing him, as we did so, to stop in front of us. "Be careful," I began, "there's a man in the woods he might be dangerous." I've no idea why I said that, the words flowed from me seemingly on autopilot.

"What? What do you mean?" Stammered the boy in response.

I repeated the statement with an intensified urgency, "There's a man in the woods he might be dangerous." The twins, who stood behind me like bodyguards, remained silent.

The boy answered defiantly, "There's nobody there, let me through."

Suddenly my hand flew through the air colliding with the boy's face as I delivered an almighty slap, his lard filled cheek rippled with the impact nearly making him fall from his bike, "Insolence." I shouted at the same instant my palm struck his cheek. To a passing bystander I must have looked like a Nazi interrogator striking his victim about the face with a leather glove. We rode off without another word being spoken leaving the bemused boy to contemplate what had just happened to him.

Please keep in mind I was very young at the time this occurred and would not dream of or condone doing something like that today. I think that probably ranks as the worst thing I've ever done to another human being in my life and that includes what happens in the story below.

I lived in Acacia Road Brantham literally two minutes away from Brookside Primary School. Down the street from us lived another family with two sons around my age called Terrance and Phillip. I don't remember much about their parents except to say that before they moved away there was a local scandal after their mother had an affair with another parent in the village, they ran off together abandoning her family in the process. With the local primary school being located pretty much at the end of our road it goes without saying that as well as being neighbours Phillip, Terrance and myself attended the same school which is where we became acquainted.

The day had started out ordinarily enough. I'd left the house first thing in the morning on my bike to meet the twins who lived less than five minutes away from me on Palfrey Heights. I was the self-appointed leader of our little group, which pretty much just meant that I got my way whenever we were deciding what to do or where to go. Juice, Stu and I had been riding around the village on our bikes for several hours when, starting to get bored and tired, we returned to Acacia Road and parked our bikes by the street sign at the entrance to the cul-de-sac. As we stood their discussing what to do next, we noticed Terrance and Phillip playing outside their house.

There had been a time when Terrance and Phillip were my friends but I found them pretty annoying and it hadn't been long before we'd fallen out. I cannot for the life of me remember the catalyst behind our falling out but by then it did not matter, we were bitter enemies and their very presence in the road annoyed me beyond words.

When our two groups spotted each other a war of words broke out that became progressively more heated. As I shouted across my next quick-witted jibe at Terrance behind me the cool hand of fate was at work, well, one of the four identical hands of the twins were anyway. I heard Juice's voice behind me, "Chris, look at this," he said urging me to turn around. I didn't respond, I was too involved in the argument. Juice persisted, "Look what I've got." I sighed and turned to face him annoyed that I'd been interrupted in the process of delivering what could only be described as a sick burn.

"What is it?" I asked without hiding my annoyance. In Juice's left hand he held a stick. It was a good stick about thirty centimetres in length, not too crooked, a nice balance to it, it was without question a strong stick. The stick however was not the part I should focus on because at the end of the sick Juice had impaled the mother of all dog turds. I mean this thing was huge and judging by the moist appearance of it probably pretty fresh too, still despite the size and freshness it held it's form on the end of the sick, there was zero chance of droppage. Through the air I could almost taste the pungent aroma emanating from the dog log as I pulled my t-shirt over my face to block the worst of it while we spoke. I glanced at Stu, there was an expression of disgust on his face mixed with a curiosity for what might happen with this foul device in our possession. It seemed to me I didn't have a choice, I reached out my hand and said to Juice, "Give me the stick."

Juice looked at me. Suddenly he seemed worried, "What are you going to do?"

"You'll see," I told him, "give me the stick." Several seconds passed, neither of us moved an inch, I repeated my demand again in a more authoritative tone, "Juice. Give me the stick."

With a tremble in his arm Juice reached over and carefully placed the stick in my hand. I turned to face Terrance and Phillip holding my new weapon high above my head. "What are you going to do?" Stu asked. I did not reply. Instead I began to cycle towards our adversaries. It was only a short distance I had to ride towards where Terrance and Phillip stood probably taking all of ten seconds to complete if that, not much time to think at all. The brothers to their credit stood firm as I approached, I was brandishing my stick in full view but they failed to notice that the end of the stick, although brown, was not branch at all but another substance entirely. I charged directly for Terrance who was standing legs apart trying to look as tough as he could in the road. It was, as far as he was concerned, a game of chicken and he was determined not to be the one to move. Within seconds I was upon him, Terrance didn't flinch but at the last second, I swerved and swiftly looped around behind him, as I did so I dragged the stick down his back and rode quickly off to rejoin my friends who had come in slightly closer to watch events unfold. I turned back around to face the brothers alongside my friends holding the now deuce free stick by my side approximately six feet away from the soiled Terrance.

"Oh, that's hard," Terrance said completely unaware of what exactly had happened to him, "stroke a stick down my back I'm really scared." His sarcasm wasn't lost on me. I smiled at him and responded with six little words and a smile.

"There was shit on that stick!"

Terrance scoffed, "Yeah right, of course there was." I tossed the stick to the side and held up my hands as I shrugged. I didn't feel the need for any more words.

Phillip walked behind Terrance and looked at his brother's back, "Urm…" he spoke hesitantly as if he was concerned for his brother's reaction after confirming my statement, "There was shit on it."

Terrance froze, the information taking a few seconds to register in his brain. "What?" he replied.

"There was shit on it," Phillip repeated, "there's shit all down your back."

I have never heard a sound come from another human being like the shriek made by that soiled little boy but it is probably best described as very loud, extremely high pitched and pretty ruddy feminine. Terrance clawed at his t-shirt trying to get it off as fast as possible as he ran back to his house caked in feces and calling for his parents. The twins and I rode out of Acacia Road in hysterics shouting classic zingers back at the brothers as we went, things like "Don't shit yourself Terrance", you know proper quality jokes, no cheap shots. We laughed so hard it was difficult to stay on the bikes while we rode to Juice and Stu's house where we felt we would be safe until the heat died down. We knew there most definitely would be heat, there had to be for high jinx of this calibre. A few minutes later we arrived at Juice and Stu's house, we dumped our bikes in a pile on the front lawn and made our way inside still laughing our heads off. It was probably only five minutes after that when we heard the phone ring and then less than a minute after that when the twins mother knocked and then poked her head around their bedroom door.

"Chris," she said softly, "that was your father, he wants you home now." My friends and I exchanged glances; that was fast.

I left my friends' house and biked home where I was met by my parents who were waiting at the door. Nervously I got off my bike and went inside where my father proceeded to tell me how moments after the twins and I had left the street there had been a knock at our front door. My father had opened the door to a white t-shirt held up in front of his face, a white t-shirt that was, of course, smeared with dog excrement. "DO YOU KNOW WHAT THIS IS?" yelled the t-shirt aggressively. My father was shocked, imagine opening the door to an excrement covered t-shirt not knowing anything about the chain of events that brought it to be there.

The t-shirt lowered revealing the very annoyed face of Terrance's dad from down the road, "THIS…" he said his face red with anger, "THIS IS SHIT!". It was at this point I realised how lucky I'd been. Had this outraged parent come over and explained what had happened calmly and told my father how his son had maliciously and with intent, smeared his son with dog shit I would probably been in a fair amount of trouble but because in his anger he was so funny my father couldn't help but see the funny side himself, so much so that I don't even remember being punished, I think I was just sent to my room. My father told the story for years to come doing his own impression of a furious Terrance's dad screaming "DO YOU KNOW WHAT THIS IS?" much to everyone's amusement.

Christopher Moore

Strawberry Potato

High school was not the best time in my life. I became a target for bullies and spent a lot of time trying to fake an illness in order to avoid having to go into school but despite my high school experience ending up this way that's not how it started out and there were even a few good times and funny little scrapes along the way.

I remember one maths lesson in which I'd gotten on the wrong side of the teacher somehow and after telling me off she wanted to convey the point that what I had done wouldn't be forgotten so she told me "I'm like an elephant. I will never forget." It was in the middle of that statement she paused, I can only assume for dramatic effect so after she said, "I'm like an elephant." I responded quickly and without thinking.

"What you've got big ears and a trunk?" The whole class erupted with laughter however my teacher did not see the funny side at all for some reason.

Although I wasn't always successful at avoiding school one thing I always avoided while I was there was PE. I managed to go the last two years at that school with only maybe one or two lessons where I had to take part. I achieved that by getting my parents to write the occasional note to excuse me from PE and then forging copies of those notes so in the event I couldn't persuade anyone to write a new one I had a forgery as a backup plan. The funny thing was it wasn't even that I didn't like PE, I never had anything against exercise, it was the teacher I didn't like who I'll refer to here as Mr. P. Mr. P was a strange looking man, not only was he very tall and goofy looking but he was one of those men who simply refused to admit he was bald and instead fully committed to the comb over. Of course, the comb over did not fool anyone and in the slightest breeze it flew off to the side flapping around like a horizontal air dancer further highlighting the man's desperation to make people believe he still had hair. Still all this would have been fine, the real problem was at the end of the lesson Mr. P liked to stand by the boys' showers and watch all the boys go in, you know, just to make sure everyone was washing properly. "Come on boys," he'd say, "wishy washy." Call me crazy but even at the time that seemed like a red flag, every time I heard those two creepy words it sent a shudder down my spine and that's why I didn't participate in PE.

Apart from home time the best part of the school day for me was lunch. I went to the canteen at lunchtime every day for dinner and queued up with everyone else. It paid to get to the canteen early because if you got there early you'd be able to get a chocolate milkshake. If you didn't get there early you'd be left with strawberry and if you get there late probably only banana. I personally like all three flavours but given the choice I would always go for chocolate, what kid wouldn't? It always annoyed me that they sold out so quickly every day. If something goes quickly on a consistent basis surely it stands to reason that you should make more of that item and therefore sell more and make more money. It seemed like common sense to me yet the school never picked up on it much to my frustration. That day I hadn't got out of lessons quickly enough and so I had to settle for a strawberry milkshake. I got my lunch and sat down with my friends Juice and Stu and another boy called Andrew. Andrew wasn't really a friend as such but he was in my form and he was pleasant enough normally. He was a chubby little Asian boy and... well that's pretty much all I remember about him other than he always wore a shirt and tie which isn't saying much because we all did; it was the uniform. We sat at our table chatting and getting ready to eat but when I wasn't looking Andrew had decided to play a little joke on me. As I spoke to my friends Andrew chose his moment, took the saltshaker that had been in the middle of the table and poured a generous amount of it into my milkshake. He was seen in this endeavour by Juice and, aware of this, Andrew tried to buy his silence with a cheeky smile, a wink and the promise that the payoff of his little jape would be worth it. Unfortunately for Andrew both Juice and Stu were cowards and tell tales, this really became apparent when we were at college but even at school it was hard to rely on them if things went south.

"Chris," said Juice without a moment's hesitation, "don't drink your milkshake, Andrew has poured salt in it." I picked up my cup and looked inside, I couldn't see anything, it had either been a very small amount or it had dissolved into the liquid, nevertheless I was annoyed. I liked my milkshake. I wanted to drink it. I most definitely did not want Andrew to pour salt in it thereby ruining the delicate taste balance made by combining both milk and shake. Further to that I really did not care for the smug expression on Andrew's face as he chuckled to himself like a mischievous chipmunk. He sat on his chair ready to tuck into his jacket potato that was still pristine and untouched on his tray. His lunch was intact. Mine was now tainted.

'Right,' I thought to myself, 'he's not getting away with this, that milkshake is the highlight of my school day. It's my treat. It's my favourite thing. If I can't have my milkshake then you're damn sure not having your potato'. Without saying a word and like a stone-cold potato assassin, I took my milkshake and poured the goopy bright pink liquid over his entire jacket potato. Andrew sat there open mouthed unable to believe what I'd just done to him.

"What did you do that for?" He asked perplexed, "there wasn't even much salt in your drink, it would've still been fine. I can't have any lunch at all now. You're going to be in so much trouble."

As if on cue the strictest and most feared teacher in our school strode through the canteen, Andrew saw him and the smug smirk quickly reappeared on his lips, "You're for it now, I'm telling."

- Now I really was worried, if he did in fact snitch as he planned, I would be in a lot of trouble. I probably wouldn't get to eat my dinner either and damn it, I was hungry. Andrew raised his hand. He was only bloody doing it. He was going to drop me right in it. The strict teacher's path to get his lunch took him right past our table, there was no way he was going to miss Andrew's outstretched hand and sure enough he didn't. "Sir…" Andrew began before being abruptly silenced by a quick gesture to shush by the stern teacher. Andrew did as he was told and abandoned his sentence after the first word. The teacher leaned over the table and studied the potato on Andrew's tray which sat there covered in its brand-new pink marinade, "Hmm," he said thoughtfully, "that looks interesting, I might have that too." Before Andrew could venture a word of protest the teacher spun around on his heels and carried on making his way to the lunch line, presumably to quiz a confused dinner lady on the tasty looking pink sauce they were using on their potatoes. I smiled and tucked hungrily into my dinner.

Christopher Moore

Where There's Foam...

After high school was over I went on to a local college in Ipswich studying art and design. I didn't want to go further afield like a lot of people do at that age to be more independent and live away from home. The idea never really appealed to me. I pictured living with a bunch of messy students, eating beans for every meal and washing my own pants and thought no thanks, that's not for me. I wasn't ready to wash my own pants yet. I was still young. The reason I decided to study art and design was simple. Before I left high school, I'd had a meeting with a career's advisor, this is a person whose chosen career obviously hasn't turned out the way they expected so instead they travelled around schools telling children what they could or couldn't do with their lives. Advice on how to get into your chosen profession from a man who couldn't get into his seemed, even at that time, pointless. I told my careers adviser I wanted to be a graphic designer, even though back then I did not have the faintest clue what the job really entailed but as I needed to say something, and as I thought it sounded pretty cool, it was the answer I ventured. No sooner had the words 'graphic designer' left my mouth than the careers advisor scoffed and told me in no uncertain words that I would never be a graphic designer and I should instead look for a more "realistic" career. Following that meeting my mind was made up. I would be a graphic designer no matter what, I just had to find out what one was first.

After high school college was a refreshing change. I mentioned before that high school wasn't a particularly good experience so when I went to college, I treated it as a fresh start, a chance to reinvent myself that I took full advantage of. Before the first term had started, I had grown my hair to shoulder length and had also grown myself a moustache. Don't get me wrong the moustache was not a good look; it was the kind you grow when you first start shaving in that middle ground between nothing and real facial hair. I kept that thing probably for about a year and despite it living there on my top lip making me look like a juvenile Tom Selleck or Burt Reynolds I found I still had no trouble attracting girls. It makes me fear for the judgement of my own daughters. Please let them stay away from idiotic boys with bum fluff moustaches. I suppose at least I eventually wised up and shaved that mother off.

Not too long into college I started hanging around with a bunch of new friends, Calvin, Simon and Harv. Calvin and I were into guitars so we decided straight away to form a band. We had several different line-ups during college under a variety of different names but only ever played a handful of gigs. Years later Calvin and I found ourselves working together at a graphic design company called Pilkington Design & Print where we reformed our little band and called ourselves 'Om Nom Bomb'.

When we started college the art and design building was not located on the rest of the college campus but instead it was a separate building on the other side of town near the Ipswich museum. The property was very old and actually closed down during our time there, it was then relocated to the main campus. Before that happened, it was a pretty cool place to study. On this particular day Calvin, Simon, Harv, the twins (who had chosen the same course as me) and myself were in that old building working on a group project. I cannot remember exactly what it was we were working on but I don't think we were concentrating too hard on whatever it was, it was more of a time filler than an important piece of coursework. For reasons known only to himself (probably just because it was funny) my friend Simon had collected the fire extinguisher from where it was stored near the exit of the room and brought it over to where we were seated.

"Chris, I dare you to hit the top of this." Simon said… without saying 'Simon says' so I should probably have known to ignore it. I didn't think for more than a second before acting. I should definitely have thought for longer or at least examined the fire extinguisher beforehand but in my mind, I didn't need to do anything of the sort because I was sure of two things.

1. The fire extinguisher couldn't go off unless the safety pin was to be removed.
2. There was no way in hell Simon would have removed that pin.

So, without a moment's hesitation I hit the top of the extinguisher as hard as I could without the knowledge that Simon had, of course, removed that very pin. I don't know if you've ever let off a fire extinguisher before but just in case you haven't let me tell you that once you set it off there's no stopping it, that thing is going to empty itself whether you want it to or not. In what seemed like a slow motion replay my fist connected with the top of the extinguisher at the exact moment I noticed the pin dangling from Simon's finger. It was too late. The lever compressed with a click and very suddenly it seemed the illusion of time slowing down had ended and I was back in real time. A mighty jet of foamy water erupted from the nozzle of the fire extinguisher and sprayed around the room wildly covering everything in its path. There was immediate panic as everyone leapt to their feet trying to escape from the water. Simon had dropped the extinguisher immediately and it lay there on the floor completely out of control quickly flooding the room. All of us, with the exception of the twins, were trying frantically to soak up the water with paper towels hoping against hope that none of our tutors would choose that moment to come into the room and check on our progress. It was as the extinguisher began to run out of water that the true extent of our situation started to dawn on us. There was water everywhere and it was obvious that no amount of paper towels was going to get rid of it any time soon. The water was running down the walls and off the desks that were all sopping wet and it was collecting on the floor that was already at least a centimetre deep. We were all naturally concerned however Juice and Stu were losing their minds. Never have I seen two people more scared about getting into trouble as those two. Not only did they want to run away but they also made it clear they would not hesitate to give us up if anyone at all asked them what had happened. Great friends huh? Everyone else pitched in to try and find a solution but in the end, there was only one thing we realistically could do. We took the fire extinguisher, put the pin back in and hung it back in its holder by the door. Then we collected our belongings, left the room and walked out of the building as if nothing had happened swearing to deny all knowledge of the incident. Well apart from Juice and Stu that was who would sing like canaries as soon as they felt under threat themselves.

A few days later there was a meeting. The head of the art and design block assembled all faculty and students, literally everyone in the art and design block into the main hall. It was there he described in full detail the mess they had found in the room we had destroyed, the amount of time it had taken them to clean the room and the cost of fire safety equipment, specifically extinguishers. My friends and I sat there exchanging worried glances. We had no idea if they knew it was us who were responsible. At any moment we could have been hauled up in front of everyone like the bunch of ne'er-do-wells we were and exposed. Not only that but at the same time Juice and Stu were saying to us in whispers "We're not going to lie," and "We'll tell if they ask us." at that point I wondered if they had a single spine between them and if they knew what it meant to actually be a friend. Eventually the meeting ended and as it turned out, nobody knew who the culprit was and nobody ever thought to ask the twins anything so we were safe.

If anyone from the local college faculty were to be reading this then I think it's important to stress that despite what I've written above… Juice and Stu did it.

Christopher Moore

Security Code

Following the fire extinguisher situation, the twins became more like outsiders than a proper part of the group because they had lost everyone's trust and respect. It wasn't just that incident either there were plenty more times they let themselves down. When we were drinking, they claimed to have drunk before we arrived and acted in a way, they thought someone drunk would act, which was incredibly over the top and convinced nobody. When's the last time you saw someone lie on a bench, hold their leg up and shout "I'm a leg," before running around all over the place like a lunatic? That sort of thing happened on too many occasions to the point that my girlfriend at the time requested that we stop hanging around with them. When we were in trouble they ran, not only when there was a fight but also, they ran at the slightest hint that there might be a fight.

There was a time when I was in a local music store with Juice, Stu and Calvin looking at the new album releases when without warning this strange woman rammed into my leg with her child's buggy and I mean rammed hard. I was standing still at the time and she just hadn't been looking where she was going however little things like facts didn't matter to her.

"Apologise then," said the woman. She was probably about thirty years old, pretty chubby with a poor complexion. Her greasy black hair was tied in a ponytail and her face was screwed up like she'd just bitten into a lemon, still the navy shell suit she wore told you this was a lady with class. Oh no wait... not "with" ... Picture Waynetta from the television programme *Harry Enfield and Chums* and you won't be too far off the mark.

I looked at her and then looked down towards the buggy, my leg still sore from the impact, "I was standing still and you hit me, I'm not apologizing."

"You apologise now or I'll get my boyfriend and he'll beat the hell out of you for stepping on my baby." She looked at me breathing heavily and red faced, pushing her child around had obviously been a bit more cardio than she was used to.

"Fine," I replied, "get him." A few moments later a wall of man appeared. I mean this guy was huge. Andre the Giant huge. And ugly too. Lemmy ugly. He could have beaten me senseless in a heartbeat and I wouldn't have been able to do anything about it. Suddenly I was worried but I stood my ground.

"You stepped on my kid now my missus is upset so you better go over there and apologise to her." He looked angry, very angry. I did not feel safe but even so I refused point blank to apologise. I looked over my shoulder, Calvin stood firm on my right looking more than a bit worried. I looked to my left, Juice and Stu were gone. Not just somewhere else in the store either, they weren't just laying low over by the vinyl or something they were gone, gone, out of the shop and down the flipping road.

"If you don't apologise to my misses I'm going to wait until you come outside and then you're dead." The angry man wasn't going to stop and he wasn't going to listen to reason, Calvin was in my ear telling me to apologise so we could get out of there but I was stubborn. I'd done nothing wrong. I'd been wronged. I deserved the apology. We went back and forth for five to ten minutes arguing the point as the giant got more and more angry. Of course, in the end I apologised, I'm not proud of doing so but it was probably the wisest thing to do in that situation if I intended to stay attached to my limbs. I apologised to the woman for existing in an area she felt she should be able to push her buggy through without paying attention to her surroundings. I apologised to her for her hitting me. I apologised to her but I made them work for it. I didn't run away and I didn't roll over without a fight. It's at times like this when you find out who your friends are though and as I stubbornly argued with a man twice my size Calvin stood next to me ready to back me up while Juice and Stu showed a longer yellow streak than an incontinent senior badly in need of a nappy. After all this Juice and Stu became less and less a part of the group and more the butt of our jokes. Yes, they still hung around with us but generally only in college and weren't often included in nights out or anything else.

During our time at college the twins and myself still lived in Brantham and had to get the number ninety-six bus into town every day. This could be an expensive business so to save money it made sense to get a bus pass which, back then, could only be purchased from the local council building in Ipswich town centre. A small group of us were walking to the council building to accompany Juice on his way to buy his bus pass. I had collected mine some weeks earlier and having never been in the council building before Juice was very keen to know where he had to go and what the process was. "Don't worry," I said, "it's simple. You'll only be inside five to ten minutes tops." I went on to explain to him what the process was in talking to reception and then going through to the correct department. "The only problem is when I went in the receptionist said I could go through and she forgot to tell me how to get through the doors so I looked like a right idiot trying to open it by myself."

Juice looked worried, "So what do you need to do then? Are they supposed to come and open the door for you?"

"No, they're not." I told him, "They have coded locks they change every day so you need to ask them for the security code to the door and they'll give you a four-digit number then you're straight through." I paused and lowered my head slightly. "I wish someone had told me that before I went in myself."

We arrived at the council building and all went inside to wait for Juice sitting patiently on some plastic chairs located just inside the door. Meanwhile Juice made his way up to the reception counter. The woman at the desk smiled at him politely as he approached, "Good morning, how can I help?"

"I'd like to buy a bus pass." Juice replied cheerfully.

"That's fine," the receptionist gestured to a door on her right, "just through there." She then turned to her computer and started getting on with the rest of her day. Juice did not make his way to the door, instead he stayed rooted to the spot and waited patiently in silence. Thirty seconds or so later the receptionist became aware he hadn't moved and confused she asked, "Is there anything further I can help you with?"

Juice replied nervously, "Yes. Sorry. Can I have the security codes to your doors please?" We all looked at each other stifling our laughter and doing our best to keep our game faces on as the bemused receptionist explained to Juice that all the doors in the building just opened with a push, just like any other door. We all walked back outside as calmly as possible before erupting into fits of laughter no sooner had our feet hit the pavement and the door closed behind us, unable to believe that he'd fallen for my ruse. I had played him like a violin.

Five minutes later Juice left the building holding his new bus pass. "You bastards," he said simply as we laughed, "you absolute bastards."

Christopher Moore

Nude

College was going really well. Calvin was the only one of us paying his own way through with a proper job working on the fish counter in a supermarket whilst the rest of us burnt through our student loans drinking and having fun. Even now I owe money on my student loan but Calvin's time with the fish, which at the time seemed much worse than a small debt, has long since passed. My parents were very keen for me to have a job also but I definitely wasn't and I made it my mission to avoid work for as long as possible. Despite my best efforts I did end up being signed up to an agency that supplied temporary staff for factories as and when they were required. Luckily for me this was before everyone had a mobile phone so making contact with me wasn't as easy as it would be today. To get in touch and offer me a shift the agency had to call and get through on my parents' landline. My parents had three phones in the house, two downstairs and one upstairs so an incoming call could be heard throughout the house. The technique I used to avoid these calls was simple, I would go to the phone upstairs and take it off the hook which would make the line busy and effectively take out all the phones in the house. It was important in doing so that at a glance the phone appeared to be exactly as it should be so I'd leave the receiver carefully balanced above the button, unless you looked very closely it would appear to be hung up properly. It was the perfect crime. Occasionally someone would notice the phone wasn't hung up properly, usually when they tried to make a call themselves but for the most part it worked perfectly and was a good system. Sure, I could have pulled the phone cord out of the wall and be done with it but that was an intentional sabotage, there's no explaining that, there'd have to be a culprit. Much better to make it look like an accident.

But I digress. College was a fun place to be. Apart from one small part of college we enjoyed it all and the small part of it we didn't like, that was life drawing. In actual fact to say we didn't enjoy life drawing isn't really fair. The lesson in itself could have been good if we were given something to draw that we didn't mind looking at for an hour or two. A bowl of fruit for example would have been fine, a nice portrait perhaps or even, as any young college lad would naturally hope for, a naked lady, that would have been absolutely fantastic. Unfortunately for us we didn't get any of those things. What we got was Sandy.

Sandy was a tall, ugly, gangly man, probably in his mid-thirties, which obviously to us seemed ancient at the time. Like the woman who hit me with her buggy, Sandy had greasy black hair slicked back in a ponytail and a very small penis. I, of course, don't know the woman with the buggy had a very small penis but I wouldn't have been surprised in the slightest to find out she did. Another penis I shouldn't have known the size of was Sandy's but that's life drawing for you and that's why if we did show up for a life drawing class then we would have to be as drunk as humanly possible before entering the room. If you missed too many lessons you couldn't pass the course so sometimes attendance was unavoidable.

Calvin and I were very drunk. We'd been in Christchurch Park all morning drinking Old Country Cider in preparation for an afternoon drawing Sandy's bollocks. I know it's not the most mature thing to do in order to be able to look at a naked man however we were in no way mature and we did not like looking at this guy's balls in the slightest. Even now I would raise an objection. Before we left the park, we had a few cans of cider remaining that we could not take to class with us so we did what any sensible person would do, we dug a hole and buried them like a dog burying a bone to come back for later. We stumbled our way back to college, a journey that took us far longer than usual in our inebriated state and we arrived a few minutes late. When we made our way into the classroom everyone else was busy setting up their easels so we did the same while our tutor explained what we would be trying to achieve in the upcoming lesson. Basically, the idea was Sandy would come out, disrobe and strike a pose which we would draw for several minutes, when the time was up Sandy would move into another pose and we would draw this over the top of the image we had just created. This process would repeat until we were told to stop. The tutor wanted us to capture the movement of the model through the overlaid images and have that be the focus of our finished piece. I stood behind my easel and tried to pull myself together as best I could. I felt dizzy and very sick. I was pretty sure that if I were to watch Sandy stand naked in a bunch of nightmarish poses then I would definitely actually be sick so I decided my best course of action would be not to look. I could just draw a figure and keep drawing over the top of it without looking. It's art and it's subjective anyway. So, when the tutor said to start, I picked up a piece of charcoal and I began. My picture started off alright, true I had no idea what pose Sandy was in but it didn't matter, we were drawing image over image so it would all merge into a messy jumble of objects anyway and by the end I wasn't even trying anymore I was just randomly scribbling shapes on the paper. After we'd been drawing for a fair while I was no longer feeling sick but instead was finding the whole thing hilarious and was laughing like an idiot to myself as I drew. Our tutor stood up and moved around the classroom looking at everyone's work and provided them with feedback on their performance. I felt her stop behind me and study my drawing carefully. After a few seconds I stood back next to her and studied it myself. It was really nothing more than a random mess of squiggly lines and bold swirling charcoal strokes. What had I done? No doubt someone whose profession it was to teach art and had spent their life studying art would see my drunken effort for exactly what it was. I gritted my teeth and waited for the inevitable.

"This one…," she paused as if deep in thought before continuing, "this one I really like." I glanced to the right and studied her face as she admired my artwork, she meant what she was saying. "I can tell you've really looked at your subject and captured the movement perfectly on the page. Well done."

I was shocked to have received such praise especially considering I hadn't even glanced in Sandy's direction once the entire lesson but that's the thing about art, it's open to interpretation.

Salt

This story is possibly the most stupid and dangerous thing I have ever done in my life bar none, so much so that I'm actually hesitant to write about it. I think if either Calvin or myself had taken even a few seconds to properly think about what we were doing then this would never have happened. Unfortunately, though it did happen and so I have no choice but to include it here.

It all started when Calvin got himself a video camera and came up with the idea to create his own version of the MTV program *Jackass* that he named *Numbnuts*. *Jackass* was a show featuring a group of guys doing various extreme stunts and pranks that were often dangerous and / or flat out disgusting. Not that we did it at their level of stupidity, we didn't... well apart from this one occasion.

It was a weekday, Calvin and myself had finished college for the day and taken the bus to my parents' house in Brantham. My parents were both at work and my sisters were both still at school so apart from us the house was empty. We were trying to come up with something decent to film for *Numbnuts Three* but it was proving more difficult than expected. We'd done a lot in episodes one and two so it was getting harder to think of fresh ideas. A few examples of things we'd done in the past would be we'd mimed 'Son of a Preacher Man' and filmed it as a comical music video, we'd shot condoms filled with water off a bird feeder with an air pistol and we'd put an electric muscle stimulator on Calvin's head and gradually increased the current. Apparently, you can feel the electricity in your teeth.

In a last-ditch attempt to find inspiration that day we decided to watch some footage Calvin had captured in the previous week or so. The decision to watch that tape resulted in a series of snap decisions and a result neither of us would ever forget. The exact contents of the video we watched I do not remember but there was something on there involving one of his friends eating some sugar.

"What's the point of that?" I asked Calvin, "Anyone can sit there and do that. I could top that easily."

Calvin looked sceptical, "Oh yeah, how exactly would you beat that?"

I thought for the briefest of seconds, "I could drink salt…"

We looked at each other. That was it. Inspiration hit us like a bolt of lightning. We hurried downstairs. There was a nervous excitement in the air as we searched through my mother's kitchen for the seasoning we required. We should have been considering the consequences. We should have at the very least questioned whether or not there was any actual risk involved. In fact, the idea should have been written off before we even went downstairs but somehow it wasn't. Somehow it seemed like the best idea we'd ever had and there was no doubt in our minds it was going to be amazing.

"Got it," I cried triumphantly as I held the large tube of salt aloft. I opened another cupboard and picked up a glass as Calvin began filming. I opened the salt and proceeded to fill the glass. There didn't have to be much salt in the glass for it to look like a lot but soon I had a good shot of salt in there. I kept pouring. The glass reached a quarter full.

"That's a lot." Calvin commented as I kept pouring. Soon the glass was half full. I put the tube of salt down on the counter and picked up the glass. It did look like a lot of salt. It was a lot of salt. I stared at it and swirled the glass like a wine connoisseur getting ready for a tasting. For the first time I hesitated. It really was a lot of salt. Calvin was also becoming unsure. A tense atmosphere had descended upon the kitchen and even though it had it still felt like there should have been more tension, some fanfare, a drum roll at the very least, there wasn't anything of the kind. Instead Calvin nervously broke the silence with a question.

"Are you really going to drink all that?" he asked nervously still pointing the camera at me. I paused for a second taking a last look at the half full glass of salt before raising my head and looking directly into the camera.

"Yeah, I am." I didn't wait to see if Calvin had any follow up questions or maybe even a word of caution. Instead I lifted the glass to the camera, "Cheers," I said with an unjustified confidence before I swiftly raised the glass of salt to my mouth and took it down like it was a shot of vodka.

As soon as the salt hit the back of my throat, I regretted my decision. Instantly my throat closed as if an invisible pair of hands were crushing my larynx. All of the moisture in my mouth was absorbed in a heartbeat. I thought about what happens when you pour salt on a slug or a snail and wondered why that hadn't entered my mind before it was too late. I choked gasping for air. My eyes bulged out of my skull. I was gripped with a blind panic. In that moment it occurred to me that I might even die. As I fought desperately for air a fountain of salt flew back out of my mouth, I stumbled around the kitchen coughing, spluttering and spraying salt everywhere I went covering the floor and surfaces in it before I fell to my knees in the middle of the cold tiled floor. In that state it was impossible to speak. The only thing in my mind was water. I knew had to get to water as soon as possible but despite there being a tap only six feet away from me actually getting there seemed like a gargantuan task. Calvin, seeing I was in real distress, stopped filming. This upset me even more. I was dying for his flipping movie and now he wasn't even filming it. I stopped trying to cry out for water and instead tried to tell him to keep filming. Yes, I was that stupid, but it didn't matter as I couldn't make a sound anyway, as far as he was concerned, I could have been asking for anything even something ridiculous like more salt. Calvin hoisted me up and helped me to the kitchen tap where I began rinsing my mouth out. I leaned over the tap, took a mouth full of water, swirled it around and spat it out over and over again. The salt didn't want to come out but after about ten minutes my mouth was at least clear enough to be able to actually swallow some water. My throat was in extreme pain and every time I swallowed it hurt like hell still, I gulped down as much water as I could, glass after glass for what seemed like an eternity until eventually, I was able to speak again even if it was only a whisper.

"What did you turn that camera off for?" Were the first words I croaked to Calvin. He laughed in relief.

"Mate I thought I was going to have to call an ambulance." I stifled a laugh that turned into a cough. I had consumed a lot of water by this point but I could still only taste salt so with my next few glasses I added in some orange squash to try and counter that sickening flavour.

The kitchen was a complete mess, there was salt literally everywhere and I knew if my parents were to come home and see it not only would I be in trouble for the state of it but also, I would have to offer some sort of explanation. Finding a reason, the kitchen was covered in salt would not be an easy task so Calvin and I set about cleaning it up. The cleaning took a while but eventually we were satisfied that you couldn't tell anything had ever happened. Relieved I turned to Calvin, "Smoke?"

"Definitely." He replied. I poured out another glass of orange squash and we went outside the front of the house for a well-deserved cigarette. Unfortunately for me after what it had been through my throat wasn't quite ready for smoke. Quickly I began to feel very sick indeed.

At the top of my road lived a really pretty girl called Emma, I'd always had a bit of a thing for Emma although she'd never taken any real interest in me turning me down on the one occasion, I'd been brave enough to ask her out.

When the sickness took hold of me Emma had just come out of her house with her mother. We watched as they got into their car knowing their end of the road was a dead end so to go anywhere at all they had to pass us. Suddenly I heaved and my mouth filled with liquid, my mind raced, instinctively I swallowed but the liquid came straight back up refilling my mouth. I could not let Emma see me throwing up. Each time my mouth filled I forced it back down as her car slowly reversed out of their drive and made its way towards us. 'Drive faster' I thought to myself repeatedly in a desperate effort to will them past me. The car approached at a crawl as I did my best to act casual in the face of adversity. Emma looked out the window making eye contact with me and I raised my hand in a gesture of recognition as the car went past before, at long last, she disappeared around the corner. As soon as Emma was out of sight, I was sick.

The word 'sick' really doesn't do this experience justice, Firstly I hadn't eaten a thing so there was no partially digested food coming out of me this was pure water and I went off like a human fire extinguisher in a college classroom. As the water rushed from by body the only thing I could think was 'why isn't Calvin filming?' but I couldn't convey this to him as there wasn't a long enough gap in the expulsion process. After some time had passed the water stopped coming out of me yet I did not feel better. Calvin was asking if I was alright but something else was stirring inside me preventing me for responding, I was going to be sick again. This time what left my body was not water at all, this time it was nothing but the pure undiluted orange squash. Somehow it seemed as though the two liquids had completely separated in my stomach and come back out individually. It was quite a thing to behold. Calvin was particularly amazed however at the time I could not appreciate the majesty of the moment myself because squash does not taste very good in reverse, especially undiluted. It was a disgusting experience. It took days before I could swallow without being in pain and weeks for my voice to return to normal. It was a harsh reminder to always think before you act, a lesson that I'm surprised I've forgotten many times since.

Christopher Moore

Gothic Catherine Wheel

During college we met a guy called Ash. I don't think I ever knew his last name but Ash was a Goth. It feels a bit silly describing a Goth to you because much like the Chinese, they all look the same. Even so for those of you that might be unaware Goth's generally have very pale skin, dyed jet-black hair that is often unwashed and black clothes. No colour. Goth's don't do colour. Anyway, Ash was alright, a bit weird but alright. He went out with a girl called Janine right after I dated her while at the same time, I had quickly moved on to Janine's friend Stephanie, back then it was rare for my relationships to last more than a few weeks at a time. I don't remember much about Janine except she was a punk rock sort of girl and she tasted of spaghetti hoops, which was a pretty weird thing, I never asked her why but I guess the obvious explanation would be that she ate a lot of spaghetti hoops. It was after Ash started to date Janine that we started talking to him because we were hanging around with the same people, in fact he was even at college with us. I don't know what ever happened to him after this story takes place because this is my final memory of him so maybe he just avoided us after this. I definitely would have.

We'd left college for our lunch break and headed into town for some food and a bit of a wander around. There were three of us, Calvin, Ash and myself and for some unknown reason Ash was walking out in front of us while

Calvin and I walked behind having a conversation. We walked through town and headed into the Tower Ramparts shopping centre; we didn't have a particular destination in mind we were simply killing time before we had to return for our next class in the afternoon. I was playing with my lighter waiting to get back outside so I could smoke when it occurred to me for no reason whatsoever that perhaps it would be funny to pretend to light Ash's hair on fire just to see the look on Calvin's face as I flicked the lighter on behind Ash's back. Ash had on a black leather coat that almost reached the floor and his long black hair flowed behind him running onto the leather. I sparked the lighter into life right behind Ash just missing his hair and laughed. Ash didn't notice and carried on walking through the shopping centre with no idea what I was doing.

"Careful," said Calvin who appeared to be worried while at the same time trying not to laugh himself. I did it again closer to his hair this time, so close it almost caught him. We both laughed this time. Ash was still completely oblivious to our high jinx and continued to walk calmly in front of us. I sparked the lighter again. This time the flame touched his hair and with a quiet whooshing sound it ignited. I had just set fire to a Goth.

"Shit," said Calvin in a quiet panicked voice, "shit, shit, he's on fire!" We looked at each other both unsure about what to do. It was like a scene from a cheap vampire film in which the sun had touched upon the vampire causing him to burst into flames. That's what it looks like when you set fire to a Goth, low budget horror.

"Shush, let me think…" I paused; my mind was blank. The flames were growing at speed. It had only been done a little bit on purpose, I didn't think it would go up the way it did, as quickly as it did. Nobody could be angry for something that was mostly an accident, could they? I could feel the warmth from the flames as we continued to make our way through the shopping centre as naturally as possible. Imagine walking past this guy on your way around the shops just nonchalantly going about his day with his head ablaze. Nobody said a word to him.

"You've got to tell him!" Calvin's voice was urgent now. He was right, I did have to tell him… or… I could wait until he notices. He was bound to notice eventually. Calvin was right though we did have to tell him, it was the right thing to do after all he was losing an alarming amount of hair by this stage.

"You tell him," I said in a hushed voice.

"No, you tell him," Calvin replied angrily, "I didn't set him on fire!" That was true he didn't. He certainly had me there, still though, my word against his… no, I had to do it.

I tapped Ash on the shoulder, "Mate, I'm not sure what happened but you're on fire."

For a moment there was no reaction, Ash thought I was joking and he laughed. He was sure it was definitely a joke, how would have been on fire? It was ridiculous. Behind him a plume of black smoke wafted ever higher complimenting his gothic attire perfectly with its darkness. Then Ash noticed the heat. How he hadn't noticed earlier remains a mystery to me but when he noticed it everything else followed in quick succession. The heat, the smoke, the horrible stench of burning hair, he really was on fire. Ash began to spin around rapidly like a dog chasing its tail, oh how Ash spun. It was like watching a Catherine Wheel on Bonfire Night, only a really funny one. We tried not to laugh.

"Bloody hell Chris!" Ash screamed in a high pitched, adolescent, voice is breaking kind of way as he frantically tried to pat out the ever-expanding flame behind him. He continued to spin as he did so reminding me an Indian in an old western performing a rain dance, something that would have definitely come in handy in that situation. I think it was at that point I lost control and started to laugh hysterically. I know it was bad but I couldn't help myself. It was funny. Once the flame was out Ash just stood there in silence and grumpily pulled a few burnt, smelly clumps of hair from the back of his head and looked at me crossly. "What did you do that for?"

"It was an accident." I told him between chuckles, "I'm very, very sorry."

Like I said I don't know what happened to Ash after that but I'll bet he keeps his hair short these days.

Splash Down

Thinking about all the various things we got up when we should have been at college makes me wonder if it wasn't a small miracle any of us passed our courses at all. Even though it was only art college there were times at the end of the year where I had to present more work or argue my grades up to a passing level. We all did. Maybe art college isn't as easy as people would have you believe or maybe we should have been applying ourselves more to the work in the first place. It's probably the later if I'm honest.

It was early June around noon and a scorcher of a summer's day. We were out of college and having a drink in Christchurch Park wondering what to do with the rest of the day. Thinking back on it we used to drink quite a lot. Cider was probably what we had more than anything because it was cheap, brands like White Lightning and Old Country that didn't taste great but did the job. I still can't drink normal apple cider after having so much of them at college. Flavored ciders like Strawberry & Lime I can't get enough of but ones that just taste of apple I've gone off completely. I also used to drink a fair amount of Newcastle Brown Ale, mainly because my favourite musician Ginger Wildheart of *The Wildhearts* used to drink it. It's not the best reason to choose a drink but to be fair I remember enjoying it, although it did play havoc with the stomach the next morning. The other drink of choice for a few of us at college was something called Mad Dog 20/20 because once again it was dirt cheap and it had a higher alcohol percentage so it'd get you drunk quicker. It came in a variety of flavours, none of which were particularly nice but if you could force it down it was a good way to start a night out.

We'd been in the park for a little while and were a few ciders deep when somebody, I don't remember who, suggested we have a water fight. Just outside the park was a little off license that sold a variety of random items including water bombs, we'd seen them in there when purchasing our drinks and so we went back and got ourselves several bags of them. With the water bombs purchased we split into two teams, it was as far as I remember, Calvin, Simon and Harv against myself and the twins, I drew the two shortest straws there. We filled our water balloons in the public toilet and then went on the hunt for the other team. The park is a fair size and there were a number of places they could be so we searched the obvious places with no luck at all.

It wasn't too long before we were back outside the toilets where we had filled up the balloons in the first place. Maybe they're in there filling up more ammunition we thought. It seemed like a reasonable enough idea at the time. We went inside cautiously and looked around. At first glance the bathroom seemed empty but then I noticed at the far end the stall was closed. Somebody was in there. It must be them I thought not even considering an alternative, not even considering that it might just be some poor soul who was passing and needed to use the toilet. In my head the absurd idea that three of my friends had decided to squeeze themselves into a single dirty toilet cubicle simply to hide from us made much more sense because that's what people to when they want to go off the grid isn't it? They go to the nearest toilet and pile themselves in. We'd looked everywhere so where else could they possibly be, it was them, it had to be. I crept into the bathroom stealthily, making my way to the closed stall. I gestured silently to Juice and Stu like a soldier on maneuvers, "They're in there." We had them now, they were cornered. We readied ourselves, took aim and launched our attack throwing multiple water bombs over the top of the stall which exploded cascading water down onto the person or persons below.

"What the fucking hell is this?" A very aggressive sounding angry voice boomed out from the stall, "Who the fuck is out there? I can't even take a fucking shit!" I think it probably goes without saying that this was not the voice of any of our friends. We had just bombed a complete stranger who had just popped in there to take care of business and thereby wandered unwittingly into our battlefield. Our reaction was of course to get out of there as fast as possible before the angry man had the chance to wipe and give chase. So, laughing our heads off we ran out of the bathroom and straight into Calvin, Simon and Harv.

"So," I said out of breath, "you're definitely not in the toilets then…"

"Urm, no, of course we're not," Calvin replied.

"We need to get out of here," I hurried them out of the park before we explained what we'd done. Part of me wished we'd stuck around to see who came out of the bathroom and what sort of state they were in. Moist is probably a fair guess. Moist and angry.

Bush & Hole

Festival weather is famous for being more than a little bit dodgy, I was lucky with Glastonbury as both years I went in 1999 and 2000 it was not only hot and sunny but the lineups were great too. The best memory I have of Glastonbury 2000 was being sat at the top of a hill on the right of the Pyramid Stage smoking a cigarette and watching David Bowie headline, that was truly a once in a lifetime experience. Back then I was dating a girl named Rachel who had originally been a friend of my sisters until I stole her away for myself. We went to Glastonbury with Rachel's father and, in 1999, her best friend Ellie. It was a complicated time for me in the build up to the 1999 festival, I was with Rachel but Ellie and I had kissed in Rachel's kitchen a week or two previously after we'd been to see *Human Traffic* at the cinema and the tension between us was obvious to everyone except Rachel. Rachel's dad had even noticed, I think it's fair to say he wasn't my number one fan… and I had to share a tent with him. This was the first time I had been to a festival and I was loving every second. We arrived, found a suitable camp site and put up our tents. No more than five minutes after that I'd spent most of the money, I had with me on weed but it was ok, I didn't plan to eat much as I wanted to avoid the bathrooms as much as possible. All I needed was enough money to drink because luckily us guys can pee anywhere, as an unsuspecting guy I went to school with was about to find out.

There were so many bands I wanted to see that year and I saw most of them, bands like Fun Lovin' Criminals, Straw, Ash, Travis (the only time it rained all weekend was during 'Why Does It Always Rain On Me?' in their set), Gomez, Feeder, Fatboy Slim, Kula Shaker, Annie Christian, Muse, Coldplay, Gay Dad and Dogstar (just because Keanu Reeves was in the band). If you've never heard of Straw their album *Shoplifting* was released on my birthday in 1999 and I highly recommend checking it out. The one disappointment of Glastonbury that year was Ian Dury & the Blockheads having to cancel their set due to illness.

On day one Rachel and myself had forced our way to the front of the crowd at the Pyramid Stage to watch Bush and Hole. The comical genius of having those two bands together on the bill was not lost on me, someone did that on purpose and that person is a bonafide legend. After jumping around to Bush, we stood at the front patiently waiting for Hole. Rachel was leaning on the barrier and I was behind her with my hands around her waist looking around at the rest of the crowd when I noticed the guy next to Rachel was hitting on her. With so many people squashed together he'd probably assumed she was alone or with friends, in the years before everything was done with dating applications you had no choice but to talk to girls and hope they didn't have a boyfriend close by who could do you any serious harm. Rachel was in the process of shooting the guy down but it seemed he wasn't getting the message so I leaned in and interrupted, "Back off her mate she's with me ok," I said in as friendly a way as possible, the guy turned and looked up at me.

"Holy shit," he said, "Chris?" Yes, somehow at the front of a crowd of thousands of people at the Glastonbury festival I had run into someone I knew. The guy in question was called Morris and we'd gone to Eastwood High School together, in all honesty I hadn't liked him then and I liked him even less when he was trying to crack on to my girlfriend still I decided it was nice to be nice and I made polite conversation with him hoping it wouldn't be too long before Hole took to the stage and I could go back to ignoring him. The conversation dragged on, Rachel hadn't said a word for a while and I was fast running out of things to say when all of a sudden Morris let out a loud shriek. It was a strange moment, at first glance there was no apparent reason for his mid conversational outburst or why, following the primal howl that had escaped his lips moments previously, he stood rooted to the spot with his mouth open in complete and total shock. The scene in front of me was like recreation of *The Scream* by Edvard Munch with a larger crowd or maybe, even more accurately, the aftershave scene from *Home Alone*. It was a surreal moment but the look on his face was priceless falling somewhere between abject horror and total disbelief.

"What's wrong with you, you lunatic?" I asked him creating as much distance as possible between him and us, which is not an easy thing to achieve with thousands of people pushing forwards behind you.

"The guy behind me…" Morris paused as if he was worried that finishing the sentence would confirm the reality of his situation, "he's peeing on my leg."

"Fuck," I said stifling a laugh, "well don't just let him do it then!" Morris lowered his head and stood there unmoving as the crowd around him parted trying their best to avoid any potential splashback. The time for Morris to defend himself had long since passed and he allowed the unnamed man to calmly finish using him like a tree at the roadside without and sort of protest. After that Morris disappeared into the crowd and I never saw him or spoke to him again. I hope for his sake he'd brought plenty of spare clothes and wet wipes with him. I couldn't help but wonder what became of Morris in the hours that followed and, although I genuinely hoped he was alright, I pictured him walking through the festival gates wearing only a small pair of Y-fronts on his bottom half having been forced out of sheer discomfort to discard his soggy trousers. I pictured a broken man completely alone in a sea of humanity, his head hung low and his spirit broken while his damp legs smelt strongly of Sugar Puffs. I felt sorry for Morris and I hoped that whatever the sequence of events was following his disappearance, it wasn't long before he found his way to a shower and a fresh pair of trousers.

Ever since then I've been pretty wary of attempting to get to the front at a festival. It's hard to get there in the first place and obviously if you manage it the people around you might not want to give up their spot just because they need a little thing like a toilet so there's always a risk of being Morrised. If you do want to get to the front at a festival the easiest way is probably to light a flare, someone did that right next to me and my friend Jason at the Download festival 2012. The man who did it got an instant path to the front to see The Prodigy, probably because everyone close to him was too scared of having their face burnt off not to move out of the way. How the hell he got a flare past security though is anyone's guess, Jason and myself were forced to drink all our beers at the gate because they weren't allowed in but that guy got through with a flare, unbelievable.

Christopher Moore

Amsterdam

During my college experience the opportunity arose for me to travel to Amsterdam on an educational excursion. The idea of the trip was to visit the local art galleries and soak up some of the culture the city had to offer, at least that was what the college's idea of the trip was, mine was slightly different. Amsterdam was an exciting prospect as it was not only the first time, I would be leaving the country but also my first holiday without my parents. Out of my group of friends it was only myself and Calvin that were going on the trip, I have no idea why but for some reason it didn't appeal to Simon, Harv, Juice or Stu which was something I couldn't understand because Calvin and I couldn't wait to leave.

We travelled to Amsterdam by ferry, it was quite a long trip but the beer was cheap and we bought a lot of it. After we'd stood on the side of the ferry and enjoyed staring out at the water for a bit we went inside, found a table and started drinking. It was just me, Calvin and around thirty cans of beer for the entirety of the journey so we were drunk before we even got close to Amsterdam, something which would probably explain why I don't remember much else about the ferry.

We docked at the port and got on the tram to the hotel. The tram was overcrowded and we were forced to stand packed into the carriage like sardines, it was so full you literally couldn't fit another person inside. Even so, at every stop along the route the doors opened to more passengers expecting to get on and at each stop those passengers were met by the same thing which, unfortunately for them, was Calvin's drunken face. Every time the doors opened Calvin would loudly slur the words, "Aaaaah you're not getting on son." laughing wickedly as the doors closed again and the tram carried on.

Before long we were at the hotel and being allocated rooms. It was three or four people to a room and as Calvin and I had nobody else to share with they put a third man in our room, someone who was travelling without any of his own friends at all. I forget his name but I do remember his face or at least the expression of fear on it as he sat silently on his bunk watching his two roommates smoke joint after joint until the room was quite literally filled with a hazy green fog. This poor guy really had only come on the trip to see the galleries and through no fault of his own he'd been placed in a room with two people who really couldn't have cared less about seeing any art. We were in Amsterdam for approximately five days and we were given an itinerary of the excursions our college group would be undertaking, daily trips to see all the sights we were meant to be in Amsterdam to see. Calvin and me, we went on precisely none of them.

The first thing we did in Amsterdam was buy weed. We went with a couple of other people from our college to a local cafe not too far from the hotel to sample the different sorts of weed they had on offer but it wasn't long before we ran into trouble. It had been a long day already and Calvin was looking more than a little worse for wear, still we sat down in the cafe and got our weed on. Calvin lit his spliff and took one puff, just one, before he opened his mouth and projectile vomited right across the cafe like the little girl from *The Exorcist* would undoubtedly have done were, she to smoke some skunk. Luckily, he didn't hit any of us or indeed anybody else with this tsunami of sick but the floor and a few of the tables were absolutely coated with stuff. Calvin wiped his mouth with his sleeve as I looked around at the state of the place. The horrible beige liquid dripped in large chunks from all the tables, chairs and even the far wall that had been caught in Calvin's path. The rancid puke from those surfaces collected into the growing pool already covering the floor, it looked slippery. At least the floor was tiled, I wouldn't have fancied trying to get that stuff out of a carpet. When I looked back the other students we'd come with were legging it out the door with Calvin stumbling chaotically behind them, I was in no such hurry to leave as I'd barely touched my joint and I wanted to finish, still if everyone else was off I figured I'd best follow if I were to have any chance of finding the hotel again so slowly I got up to join them. Some of the cafe staff had seen what had happened and were understandably not thrilled with the prospect of cleaning up the contents of Calvin's stomach. While the others had moved quickly and made it safely out of the door before the staff had time to react I, having taken my time to get to my feet, was not so fortunate. On my way to reach the exit I was confronted by a particularly irate waiter who was determined not to be left mopping up the disgusting mess we were leaving behind.

"You're cleaning that up," said the angry waiter placing his body between myself and the door preventing me from leaving.

"It wasn't me mate," I insisted, "the guy you want is halfway down the road."

"Yeah well he's your friend so you're going to clean up his mess." The waiter folded his arms and glared at me in a way that said I was up to my neck in it.

I glanced back at the horror scene behind me and gagged, almost being sick myself, it was not a pretty sight. "I've got no idea who that guy is he just sat at my table so if you think I'm cleaning up his puke you've got another thing coming, you work here, you fucking clean it." With that I pushed my way past him and fell out the door back into the cool night air. "I think we'd best stay away from that place for the rest of the trip." I laughed as we helped Calvin back to the hotel. Calvin was out like a light as soon as his head hit the pillow so I quickly left and rejoined the others for our first proper night out in Amsterdam. I'd write more about that night but all I can remember is there were mushrooms, magic ones. The next night there would be more of those to follow.

In the morning we woke up severely hungover and I do mean severely. When we felt able, we went out and got some breakfast from McDonalds which was the only place we ate during our entire stay in Amsterdam. We played it totally safe food wise not having bothered to even find out what the food was like locally before we left, we knew where we were with McDonalds and trying the local cuisine was just another thing that did not feature on our list of holiday objectives. After we'd eaten, we acquired some more weed and set about exploring Amsterdam but with no smart phones navigating our way around proved pretty tricky and we got lost more than a few times. Still we knew our hotel was the one near the wall sized poster of a man in very tight jeans squatting over a bollard so at least we had a landmark to navigate by. We wandered through the red-light district where ladies of the night stood in the windows attempting to entice us in like mermaids appearing to weary sailors at sea. Naturally we glanced in their direction once or twice but with no desire to leave Amsterdam either diseased or ripped off we kept walking.

Eventually we found the one cultural exhibit that we did have to check out while we were there, the one museum that sounded interesting, the Sex Museum. Now the Sex Museum wasn't as interesting as we'd thought, in fact quite the opposite, the only thing I remember being worth the entrance price was the wax work elderly woman that pops out on a motion sensor screaming when you walk past, that thing makes you jump out of your skin. We had a look around then left not too long after feeling a lot more shameful than we did when we went in.

We spent most of the rest of the trip in the hotel smoking weed and taking magic mushrooms much to the horror of our roommate who stayed on his bunk looking completely distraught the entire time. When we purchased the mushrooms, they had given us an instruction leaflet warning not to take them on consecutive nights because it might cause a "bad trip." We were only there for a few days though so I decided to ignore this advice, I took them every night and I paid the price. The problem with magic mushrooms is that if you do end up having a bad trip the bloody things last for around eight hours and that is a very long time to suffer. Our final night in Amsterdam I took the last of our mushrooms and proceeded to have what was probably the worst night of my life.

For the longest time I sat cross legged on the floor completely convinced I was sat upside down on the ceiling just next to the light, I wasn't sure at all how I'd gotten up there or how I was getting down but I was calm at relaxed as long as I was able to smoke. Calvin and I were talking absolute rubbish for hours but at the time it seemed to us that our conversations were really profound, I was having all sorts of realizations about my life and how I'd been wasting it. I remember I had a particularly long rant about television and how I would never watch it again as long as I lived because "It's just people pretending to be other people, it's not even real. What's the point?" I probably spent a few hours on that and I did end up watching television again as soon as the mushrooms wore off.

After I had somehow managed to climb down from my ceiling hallucination, I started to feel bad. Not bad as in ill but more mentally bad. I became extremely paranoid and without warning everything became a source of fear, I was convinced everyone wanted me dead and I was terrified. For the next few hours we sat in the room, Calvin had found a plastic disc and, as I lay on my top bunk, he swirled it around on the metal below my mattress creating a strange whooshing noise which I could not identify the source of, and it didn't help that he swore blind he couldn't either. I lay there listening to that sound slowly driving me crazy while jumping at every shadow I saw pass by the door firmly believing that at any moment some crazed assassin would burst in and make an attempt on my life, it was a trying time. As the hours passed, we got hungry and Calvin suggested to me that it might be time for another little excursion to McDonald's. I didn't know what he was thinking, it seemed to me to be the stupidest idea in the world, the streets were full of killers, killers who were looking for me and I was supposed to risk my life for a bacon cheeseburger? It was pure insanity... but then again... I could definitely eat. We grabbed our coats and got ready to leave, I stood by the door and told Calvin to wait while I checked the coast was clear. I gingerly opened the door and stepped out into the hall; all was quiet so slowly I crept further along stealthily placing one foot in front of the other until I made it to the stairs at the end of the hallway. Suddenly I heard a noise, someone was on the way up. Scared for my life I instantly turned and ran full pelt back to the room almost falling over several times in panic during the short journey. Calvin, who heard my loud steps long before my cry to "Open the fucking door." opened the door and I ran through it slamming it behind myself as I gasped for breath. I don't know how I was ever convinced to leave that room but eventually we did. I walked through the dark streets of Amsterdam with my head down and my hood up covering my face, nobody could see my face or I was convinced they all turn around to point at me screaming like in the film *Invasion of the Body Snatchers*. I peeked out from underneath the hood occasionally just to make sure we were undetected and we safely made it to our destination. I let Calvin order first, I kept my head down and stayed behind him waiting for my turn to speak.

"Hello sir what can I get you?" Came the voice of the female assistant behind the counter who had already established through dealing with Calvin that we were English and had adjusted her greeting accordingly. I took my hood off and smiled politely.

"A bacon cheeseburger meal with a chocolate milkshake please." I chirped happily. Sometimes all you need is a burger and a shake and everything doesn't feel quite so scary after all.

I left Amsterdam a total mess. During the time we were there I hadn't looked after myself well at all and was unwashed, I stank and I looked, for the want of a better word, awful. I remember walking through customs in this state, my long greasy hair covered by a beanie hat which had a large cannabis leaf on the front of it, smelling of weed and probably still with an ample quantity of mushrooms in my system. If anyone was getting stopped that day on the way through customs it was me because my appearance literally screamed 'drugs up the arse'. Luckily for me another guy in our group called Luke had dreadlocks. I think a white guy with dreadlocks must be a definite red flag because he was detained and the coach home left without him while I sailed through without a second glance.

A few hours later I arrived back at home weary but safe and sound, all I wanted to do was sleep but I smelt so bad my parents wouldn't let me in the house until my dad had hit me with the garden hose. We've all been there.

Christopher Moore

Mini Muffin

After college ended, I really didn't know what I was going to do but one thing I did know was that I had to find a job as quickly as possible. During college my bank account had become substantially overdrawn despite the fact I had a student loan and lived at home with minimal overheads to worry about, this was mainly because of my social life and my ever-expanding record collection. I was enjoying my youth and not having the money I required, at the time, was a secondary concern. The bank did not see things the same way as I did and, having noticed my lack of incoming funds, were sending me letters chasing my debt. In my adult life I've never really been one to spend money that I don't have, I've never had a credit card, I don't take out loans and if I can't afford something I do without it however when I was at college I sacrificed those rules in order to enjoy those years to the fullest. Luckily before too long I found myself a job at a supermarket, unfortunately not the same store as my friend Calvin though who worked at the Warren Heath branch, I worked at Hadleigh Road in the bakery. During the time I was employed there, which was several years, I don't think I ever really appreciated how easy the job was and how much we were able to get away with working there. When I look back now and think of all the things that went on there it seems incredible that we weren't fired. I did come close once or twice though.

My job as a bakery assistant involved many different responsibilities such as making the bread, rolls and doughnuts, packaging, labelling, filling the shelves and so on but probably the main thing I did there was eat. I ate everything. I ate cookies and cakes all the time of course; they would have been the bread and butter of the bakery were it not for the actual bread and butter. I didn't limit myself to my own department I also swapped bread for meat with the deli staff so I could make proper ham sandwiches and I cooked frozen pizzas in the bakery ovens. I even used to open the special birthday cakes we sold, cut myself a ginormous slice and throw the rest away and those things cost a tenner a pop. I should have been as big as a house but when I was young, I could eat anything I wanted and I never put on weight, something I used to take full advantage of.

The time I came closest to being fired was, of course, because I was eating the food. When you start working for this company, they tell you the food is strictly off limits and eating anything is punishable with instant dismissal, even if the food is going to be thrown away, you're still not permitted to eat it. During my time there I had seen several people fired for just that reason. I never worried about that though because the bakery had plenty of little areas where, especially when working alone in the evening, you could sit out of sight of both people and security cameras and chow down in peace. The problem was I'd been eating there so long and getting away with it that I was getting sloppy. I was brazen with my eating to the point you could argue I was showboating. In my mind I was untouchable.

It was, I believe, a Monday evening. I was working in the bakery on my own happily packing rolls whilst munching on an open box of double chocolate mini muffins. They were good mini muffins too, fresh and moist. I do love a moist muffin. The problem was the roll packing station was in full view of customers and staff, not one of my usual eating areas but I was being good, I was working and eating instead of just eating. Anyway, I had just popped another tasty mini muffin into my mouth when I heard a woman's voice behind me.

"Excuse me, why are you eating that?" she said peeping at me between the shelves. The woman was probably around forty years old with brown hair, she wore a pair of thick-rimmed glasses and looked not entirely unlike a librarian.

My mouth was full but I turned around and replied to the customer through the shelving as I hurriedly chewed and swallowed the remnants of the muffin. "Because I'm hungry." I said matter of factly as the last crumb slid down my throat. Looking back now this was probably not the best response I could have given but like I said earlier, I'd gotten cocky.

"Right." the woman snapped at me. Suddenly she didn't seem as politely inquisitive as she had when she asked me the question moments before. "Stay where you are please, I'm a mystery shopper and I need to report this to your manager."

It was a sting. I'd been stung. Panic gripped me. I was going to be fired. I needed an excuse to have eaten that mini muffin and I needed it fast. I ran out the back and grabbed a red plastic tray that I filled with the remaining mini muffins and I then placed these by the bakery entrance with a crudely made sign scrawled in black biro saying 'free samples' before hurriedly returning to the area I was caught in so to appear as if I hadn't moved. While I waited there filled with dread, I saw Shawn, one of the night shift managers, walk past the bakery and through the double doors which lead to the warehouse.

Shawn was somewhere around 50 years old and a sufferer of short-man syndrome, which simply meant because he was short in height, he was especially bad tempered most of the time and this also meant he wasn't particularly well liked in the store. As well as being short he was quite podgy with pig like features, I only ever saw him eat fried foods and was a very heavy smoker. I'm pretty sure he's dead now... unknown causes.

Anyway, Shawn walked briskly past the bakery and, seeing my tray of muffin samples out front, he stopped, picked one up, popped it in his fat little mouth and carried on. A few minutes later the mystery shopper returned with another manager whose name I cannot recall and I was taken upstairs to a vacant office. Several managers came into the room with me to grill me on the muffin-eating incident, one of which was the aforementioned Shawn who, let's not forget, did the exact same thing I did minutes after I had done it. You can imagine my annoyance as that man started a disciplinary procedure against me having committed the same crime himself in my presence. I wanted to tell everybody he had done it too. I wanted to tell them they could check the surveillance camera because he'd done it in plain sight and would have been recorded doing so. I wanted to punch him in the face. I did none of those things. Instead I sat and took it because I'm not one to snitch on anybody no matter how much I dislike them and also, I'm pretty sure that had I punched him in the face I would have been dismissed instantly. I wasn't in the office long before they told me I was being suspended for a week on full pay. At least that was something, I would probably be fired in a week's time but at least I'd be paid up until then. I left the building, got in my car, turned up the stereo and headed to my girlfriend's house to tell her the news.

At that time, I had met and was dating a girl called Jadie who I would eventually marry and have my beautiful daughter Faith with. Jadie was an attractive blonde who, looking back on pictures from the time, was much better looking than me, I was definitely punching above my weight but if you're going to marry you should always marry up.

I spent the following week searching for another job and had successfully lined up an interview at another bakery before returning for my disciplinary hearing. During that time my dad, who always does his best to help, had written me a letter to hand to management explaining how sorry I was etc. I read the letter. I hated it, in fact I hated it so much that occasionally even now I think about it and it makes me feel sick. It was a spineless begging letter and I did not want to use it. The line in it that I hated the most, that still haunts me to this day just said "Please don't take my job away from me." however, after arguing the toss with my old man for quite some time he convinced me that it was a normal thing someone in my position would do to save their job and I handed it in. In all fairness to him that letter probably went some way to getting me out of trouble because it made me look extremely remorseful but if I could go back and burn it instead I definitely would, I have never been one to beg.

Sitting in the manager's office I just wanted to get it over with and leave, I was completely expecting to be fired and I was absolutely fine with that I just didn't want to drag the whole thing out. Still the manager went through his speech even going so far as to hold a mini muffin up in front of my face and ask me what threat it posed to his business, I ventured that unless it had been baked around a very small yet very powerful explosive device then it probably posed little threat, the manager agreed. So, it was with our shared opinion on the danger that muffin posed the store as a whole that my job was surprising spared. I was shocked, where most people were fired, I was given a week off on full pay, I was back on the shop floor. The buffet was open once again.

Russian Roulette

As I said in the previous chapter, during my time at the supermarket I never appreciated how easy the work was or how much stuff we were able to get away with. The mini muffin incident was really just the tip of the iceberg. The bakery was full of colourful characters and there are so many little stories I could tell featuring almost every one of them, below are a selection of my favorites.

Firstly, there was Albert. Occasionally I still shop at that same store and even today some twenty years later Albert is still working there. He was a strange one, a nice enough guy but very, very strange. He was a chubby fellow about five foot nine with dark hair and a way of talking that was more mumble than it was anything else. After Shaggy released his hit song 'It Wasn't Me' in 2000, about one man asking his friends advice after his girlfriend caught him cheating and Shaggy advising him to simply state "It wasn't me." when asked. Albert used that line for everything for about a year and laughed every single time he did as if he were the funniest man in the world.

I'll never forget the time when I showed up at work and my friend Nick came running up to me as soon as I set foot in the door. "Hey Chris have you seen Albert yet today?" he asked in a hushed yet extremely excited tone, his face literally beaming with pure childlike joy.

"Nope, not yet mate." I replied while prioritising the jobs that needed doing during my shift.

"Walk around the back and look," Nick carried on practically bouncing up and down in elation, "go and look but be cool, just do a loop around, glance at him and come back." I walked around the back looking over at Albert as I did so, he stood by the back wall at the roll press making the mornings rolls. Immediately I noticed what was wrong and why Nick had sent me to see for myself, I bit my bottom lip and tried my best not to laugh as I completed my short lap of the bakery. I came around the corner back to the front of the bakery where Nick was impatiently waiting for me desperate to see my reaction, unable to contain the words he'd been dying to say any longer he joyfully sang, "He cut his own hair!" It was so hard not to just erupt with laughter, even with his bakery hat on it was impossible to miss what Albert had done to himself, his hair was literally in clumps, he looked like a dog with the mange. He'd hacked at it with scissors, realised he'd bitten off more than he could chew and, obviously unable to get anywhere to sort it between his shifts, he had to try and style it out. It… Was… Amazing…

Working in what we referred to as, and the definitely not sexual sounding, "Cream Room" was a lady called Angela. Angela was a short lady with chubby features and short brown hair, her most distinguishing feature was probably her eyes because they bulged out of her head not unlike a frog's eyes, this earned her the nickname 'The Frog'. Angela didn't have too much of a sense of humor so nobody ever called her 'The Frog' to her face, she took her job seriously and so when she was in the bakery, it was a little harder to break the rules, not impossible but a little harder. I remember one time when a bakery assistant called Saul had used the expression 'Fuck a duck' in front of her and she snapped. "First of all," she began, "I like ducks and second of all, don't use that language in front of me." Personally, I like how the defence of ducks was her first priority as if Saul intended to actually sexually assault one, I wondered what animal she didn't like and would have been acceptable to use in the duck's place, maybe 'fuck a ring-tailed lemur' for example. Who knows? The only occasion I can remember anyone calling Angela "The Frog' to her face was when a baker called Ray was working out the front of the bakery dealing with customers.

Ray was the dictionary definition of an 'old git', he must have been at least seventy years old and he was our union representative so was forever arguing with managers and bailing the rest of us out if we happened to get in trouble. In fact it was Ray who had phoned personnel for me when I got my P45 at the end of the year and noticed that my ethnic group was listed on it as 'Black African' despite the fact that I'm about as pale a white man as it's possible to be without being ginger.

Anyway, a customer asked Ray a question about the cream cakes we sold, which was Angela's department. It just so happened Angela was on the shop floor filling the shelves with cakes so Ray had said to the customer, "Nah you don't want me for that, you want The Frog." he gestured towards Angela and the customer looked over towards her curiously.

"Her name's 'The Frog?" The customer asked unsure of the information Ray had given her.

"Yeah it's fine," Ray told her, "We all call her that. She loves it. Go and ask her."

The customer looked very dubious but even so she made her way over to where Angela was knelt on the shop floor. "Excuse me," she said timidly as Angela raised her head to look at the customer, "sorry to disturb you but are you The Frog?" Angela immediately shot a thunderous look back towards the bakery where Ray was in hysterics watching. Angela was not amused.

"The Frog is not my name!" she said quietly to the customer through gritted teeth.

It was important that at all times we were polite to the customers, no matter how rude they were to us. We'd all done things to get revenge on customers like that without their knowledge because when you work in the food service industry revenge is easy. That is why one of my main rules in life is never to complain about food, never send anything back and never be rude to anyone serving it to you. Break that rule and you only have yourself to blame for whatever you end up eating. I myself served up a mean sandwich of revenge to a woman who called me every name under the sun when I refused to put her extra-large bloomer loaf through the bread slicer, and I do mean this woman was properly nasty. It was company policy, the bloomer was too big and we didn't offer slicing on them, still the woman insisted, so I took the loaf around the back to the cream room and sliced it in half with a bread knife in order to run it through in two smaller chunks. Once the loaf was sliced in half, I did not immediately return to slice the bread, instead, and I'm not proud of this, I borrowed a hole in the soft white bread with my fingers and into the freshly made hole I place my gentleman's parts. After a quick jiggle about I refastened my trousers and happily put the bread through the machine apologizing to her for the wait as I did so. Never be rude to anyone serving you food!

Ray could get away with being, shall we say, less than polite to customers than the rest of us though since he was the union representative. Although he would also get in trouble and, I believe, was eventually fired, he could push the envelope further before that happened because he knew all the loopholes in the system. There was an occasion where a lady had come to the counter and asked Ray to slice up a loaf of bread for her in our slicer, as I had done for the nice lady I mentioned above. As he did so he listened to the customer quietly and patiently as she complained about the service at our supermarket, how we, the staff, didn't know what it was like to work for a living, how we should recognise that we were "a lower class" than she was and how she felt she should be treated with more respect during her shopping experience. Ray didn't say a word through this, he sliced her bread, wrapped back up nicely, placed it on the counter in front of her and smiled, "There you are madam all done for you." The lady reached for her freshly sliced loaf and bread but before she could take it Ray snatched it back out of her grasp and angrily shouted, "NOW FUCK OFF TO TESCO!"

Peter was employed first on the Deli counter and then moved on to the bakery later. We often went out drinking together and he introduced me to my best friend Jason. I haven't spoken to Peter in many years as he got obsessed with Poland, turned into a bit of a tosser and moved over there. Before all that happened though Peter had problems with his penis that became the talk of the bakery, mainly because he was so honest about it when he had no need to broadcast the details of his genital infections to the rest of us at all, in fact I think we were all happier not knowing. He'd slept with a girl and following that he thought he had contracted something; he went to the doctors who did a bunch of tests but ultimately couldn't find the cause of it. He even showed it to a girl who worked with us so she could see just how bad it was, she returned from the experience and looked as though she was about to burst into tears, "It's so black..." she said in absolute disgust, "it's... so... black!" Peter was a white man just to be clear on how far gone it being "black" was. A few weeks later he tried to brush it all under the carpet by saying he was just allergic to the shampoo he used on his pubes. Yeah of course you were Peter.

Another baker we had there was Truman. Truman was a good guy and is another person who still works there at the time of writing this book, just under twenty years after I left. As far as I remember there were no funny stories involving Truman that took place in the bakery but I did find out rather more about him that I cared to know when my friend Amy, who also worked with us, started dating him. I never spoke to Amy much about her relationship with Truman because it didn't interest me, I'd asked Amy out myself and struck out because, unknown to me she had been seeing Truman in secret and so was already involved. Their relationship was going well for them and Amy had decided to move into Truman's place, it was while they were in the process of moving in together, I got a phone call from her.

"Hi Amy, what's up?" I said answering the phone cheerfully.

"Hey," she said sounding quite downbeat, "I'm just moving all my stuff in to Truman's place." Immediately my brain switched off a bit, it seemed like it was going to be a boring conversation and she'd called to break up the monotony of unpacking, that was until she started talking about Truman having a foot fetish. By this point it was already a weird conversation as I had no wish to know what Truman was into, personally feet creep me out and I don't understand people who enjoy them in that way at all, still it takes all sorts. Amy carried on. "So anyway, I needed somewhere to store some of my things so I decided to put them in the loft..." She paused.

"OK so you needed to put something in the loft, I don't see the problem." I replied, a few seconds went by in silence as if she were debating whether or not she should continue to the conclusion of her story.

"Chris," her voice sounded unsteady, she paused again and then she said forlornly, "He's got a giant shoe." I couldn't help it, I instantly erupted in laughter, it was so random. "It's not funny he really has," Amy plowed on trying to make me see the seriousness of the situation to no avail, the more she spoke the funnier I found it, "he's got one really big high heeled stiletto."

"He didn't want the pair?" I asked when I was able to stop laughing long enough to get the words out. Despite herself Amy let out a little laugh too. I don't think she ever mentioned the big shoe to Truman, I think she let it go and got on with things. I mean how would you even bring up the subject? Why he had the shoe and how he used it remain two of life's unanswered questions and I'm quite grateful for that fact.

Sunday's were the best days to work in the bakery, not only did we get paid double time but there were also rarely any managers around, certainly our manager Alan would never work Sundays. Sunday mornings would start with four or five of us. Two bakers who would be gone before lunch because making the bread etc. obviously had to be done as early as possible in order for it to be on the shelves and sold by the time the store shut at four. Someone in the cream room who would also be gone before lunch. Then there were the other two or three of us working until the store closed, dealing with frying doughnuts, keeping the shelves stocked and serving the customers. As, by the afternoon, anyone who had the slightest bit of authority had gone home the day would often descend into absolute chaos. The main three guys who caused the trouble were myself, Dan and David. Dan was a good friend at the time and we always had a laugh, we were both into Jay and Silent Bob films and used to sing Jay's rap from the start of *Jay and Silent Bob Strike*

Back quite often, especially when we'd had a drink. David... well David was a colleague.

We got up to so much mischief when we were left to our own devices. It was fun, we found, to throw knives into the big bags of flour out the back which were used in the baking of the bread each morning. It feels cool throwing knives into stuff like a ninja, if you've never done it before I highly recommend it. Also, as the bags were made of a heavy-duty brown paper the multiple holes, we made throwing the knives into them ruined their structural integrity, meaning that when the bakers picked up those bags to use them, they would often split causing the flour to spill everywhere. This caused many an argument because the manager, Alan, always thought it was old Ray cutting up the bags for a laugh, Ray denied it of course but things got very heated between the pair of them to the point it almost stopped being funny... almost.

The most fun thing to do on any given Sunday had to be the doughnut fights. These were the other reason I came close to being fired. On Sunday's I used to fry the doughnuts, put the jam in the middle then coat the outside with sugar. I've never been a fan of doughnuts and I really used to dislike going home stinking of them at the end of the day, not to mention the fact that the oil in the fryer, the jam machine and the sugar tray were very rarely cleaned meaning I would have definitely been put off even if I loved the things. I don't know if you've ever seen how jam gets put inside a doughnut but it's quite a fun little process. Basically, you take two doughnuts at a time and impale them on two spikes on the outside of a machine called a 'Jammer', you then hit a button which dispenses the correct amount of jam in the doughnut depending on the size of the doughnut in question. For a small doughnut you'd set the machine on number six and for a larger doughnut it was somewhere between eight and ten, let's say nine. Although nine was the highest jam setting, we would ever require that was not the machines maximum setting. The machines maximum setting was ninety-nine. I know you can see where this is going, you can picture it, holding that little doughnut in your hand, impaling it on the spike and setting the machine to ninety-nine, the maximum jam it was possible to inject into a doughnut in one press of a button. The first time you do it you feel a sense of panic about halfway through. You wonder if the doughnut will hold. You can feel it getting heavy, ridiculously heavy for a doughnut and it takes time too so you're not sure exactly how much more jam is coming. It's like holding on to a lit stick of dynamite and not knowing how long the fuse is. Obviously once you've filled a load of doughnuts with that amount of jam there's only two reasonable things you can do with them. The first is to put the occasional one in boxes of ordinary doughnuts containing a regular amount of jam so someone will buy a box then bite into that special one that will explode in a sticky mess as soon as teeth break through the doughy shell, it's doughnut Russian Roulette. The second thing you can do is to throw them at someone. The Sunday cleaner at the store was an old boy called Kenny. Kenny must've been at least eighty, the poor guy was ancient and the mess he'd walk into on a Sunday was just insane. Walls, doors, equipment and even the ceilings covered in splats and streaks of jam and sugar and not only jam and sugar, cream cakes got involved too, and the raw ingredients like eggs as well, full on whole eggs smashed left, right and center. The place looked like a warzone. It had been a warzone. We were just as messy but luckily it was not part of Kenny's job to clean us down as well, that would have been an awkward process to say the least. All credit to him Kenny sorted it out week after week but eventually he'd had enough and it was reported to management. Of course, we all played dumb and denied any knowledge of how everything came to be in that state so they couldn't prove who was responsible but we were warned that a closer eye would be kept on the bakery in future. From that moment on the Sunday afternoon food fights were officially over.

Christopher Moore

The Great Escape

It was something of a rare occasion at the supermarket that we had a work night out. This is by no means a bad thing at all, merely a statement of fact. When we did have one it was done by department and organised by the staff instead of being a proper company thing, something that made saying no substantially harder. This is the story of the only work night out I can remember having during my years employed by the company and, to be fair, it's pretty surprising I remember it at all.

I'd been a long day working in the bakery and I was absolutely cream crackered; a little bakery humour there, you're welcome. I had started at seven o'clock that morning which meant I'd been awake since five-thirty, this is an early start for anyone but you can trust me when I say it feels even earlier when you've been out drinking the night before and not gone to sleep until the early hours. I'd had maybe three or four hours of sleep and left for work not entirely sure if I was hungover or still drunk. The last thing I wanted to do was go out again after work, but it was our work Christmas meal and attendance at our little evening soiree was, unfortunately, mandatory.

There was a time in my life when going out for a work-related event didn't feel so bad at all. When I got a job with Pilkington Design & Print a few years later, Christmas parties became a thing to look forward to rather than something to approach with dread and apprehension. My boss at Pilkington Design & Print, Jack, was the best person I ever worked for, he would close down the office at lunchtime and everyone would head down the pub where the food and drink would all be paid for until closing. It always puts me in mind of old Mr. Fezziwig's Christmas parties from *A Christmas Carol*, it was that sort of atmosphere.

I sat in the car park after my shift ended contemplating the night ahead. My colleague, Macaulay, sat with me busily rolling up a joint as we spoke. At that time our plan was simply to smoke that blunt, wander down to the pub and get a pre-drink, pre-drink before meeting everyone for the official pre-drinks preluding to the consumption of a meal in a local restaurant, the chosen venue, Ask Italian. Macaulay was as enthusiastic about the evening as I was, which is to say, he wasn't. I think because people spend more time with their work colleagues than they are potentially able to spend with their families and friends, it's hard to be happy about the prospect of them encroaching on personal time too.

Macaulay was my age, give or take a year or two, slim build with messy black hair and he was known as a bit of a stoner. He'd informed me earlier in the day he had some really good weed and would sort us out for the party later if I wanted to join him in a smoke. Macaulay, who smoked weed all the time, was careful to warn me of the potency of this weed but I assured him with an unjustified confidence that I'd been to Amsterdam, and I knew exactly what I was doing.

Macaulay lit the joint and passed it to me. I raised it to my lips, took a puff and inhaled deeply. Immediately I choked. It really was strong weed, much stronger than anything I'd had in the past and I felt my eyes begin to fill with water, how foolish my bravado felt as I tried to stifle my cough. It didn't take much before my head started to spin but, not being one to admit when I'm in over my head, I carried on and finished the joint. On the walk to town I was already feeling more than rough, I could happily have gone straight home to bed but I was obligated to attend, I'd already paid for my meal and I wasn't going to let that lot devour my carefully selected pizza. I arrived at the bar and ordered my first drink hoping that it would go some way to making me feel better, it didn't and as the others began to arrive, I tried my best not to appear as ill as I felt. I basically stayed quiet and kept drinking while everyone around me chattered amongst themselves. It was a good strategy as long as nobody tried to talk to me and for the most part they didn't, or if they did, I didn't notice. Every once in a while, the sickly taste of the weed returned to my mouth, which felt unbelievably dry no matter how much beer I consumed, and in my uncomfortable silence I was certainly putting them away at quite a pace.

Eventually it was time to leave and make our way to the restaurant that was conveniently located next door. My manager, Alan, turned to me, "Come on Chris, time to go." he said hurrying me on.

I wasn't one hundred percent sure if I could stand, I needed a moment to compose myself. "I still have half a drink left here, I'll get this down and I'll be right there." I watched the rest of the bakery staff file out of the pub and thought, not for the first time, that the last thing I wanted to do was go and have a meal with these people. I downed my drink and unsteadily got to my feet holding on to the table for support as I did so. As I walked slowly to the door the thought occurred to me that I could just leave. Nobody else was left in the pub with me and they probably wouldn't even notice if I was gone. The idea made me chuckle drunkenly to myself as I stepped into the December night air. I made up my mind in that moment, I was going to do it, I was going to pull off the greatest escape since Houdini first freed himself from his Chinese water torture cell and tried not to drip on his living room carpet. The only thing between me and my desertion was the small fact I had to walk past the restaurant to get away. The restaurant front was made of glass so the chances of being spotted were pretty high indeed. Glass, being a transparent medium, provides little cover to the stealthy man about town. Still nothing would deter me from my liberation because I had two very viable options and freedom was but a heartbeat away.

 The first option, obvious when you think about it, was to go the other way. If I went the other way, I may have to walk slightly further to reach my destination but the chances of being seen in my escape would fall to zero. It's a good option. The trouble was that I was unsteady on my feet and the idea of going further than I had felt like a daunting prospect. It was alright though because I still had option number two to fall back on, good old trusty option number two would see me right and no mistake, that was the option for me. I chose option number two, crouch and run.

I crouched down ready to make my move like a sprinter waiting to hear the gunshot that signified the start of his race. Imaginary gunshot heard, I set off running as fast as my wobbly legs would carry me, I bolted past the restaurant containing my colleagues and down the road. Even though within seconds I was in the clear I couldn't stop running, although I did at least straighten up to run upright, as fun as it would have been to go the whole way in a kind of demented half squat. I don't think in my life I've ever ran as fast as I did that evening, I'd gone full Forrest Gump and I... was... running.

Within minutes I had arrived at the train station. I was still laughing like an idiot to myself as I struggled to catch my breath. I thought of the monumental feat I had just achieved, I broke the rules and got away with it, nobody was any the wiser. I felt like a king, I was free as a bird. I boarded the train and took my seat. The carriage was empty apart from a single commuter who was sitting with his back to me about five or six seats in front of me. As the train began to move my daring escape began to catch up with me. The weed, the alcohol, the unnecessary physical exertion, it was too much. Once again, my head began to spin and I lowered it between my legs as I tried to regain some composure, however, the rocking of the carriage made this nigh on impossible. I let out an audible groan as I felt the sickness building inside of me. I was reminded of the salt incident from my college days because I had the same feeling, that horrible rush of liquid filling my mouth as I tried to swallow it down. I hated that feeling with a passion because I knew all too well what followed. Unable to hold it in any longer I leant into the isle and opened my mouth, for the first time that evening I was truly glad I hadn't eaten my pizza. A good few pints of vomit, mostly liquid, landed with an ugly splash on the floor of the train. I lifted my feet to save my shoes as it began to travel, with the movement of the carriage, towards my fellow passenger. The passenger, on hearing the nauseating sounds I'd produced, had one eye on the floor and hastily moved his own feet as the waters advanced.

I exited the train in Manningtree, still a good thirty to forty minutes' walk from my parents' house in Brantham. With moderate difficulty I staggered to the end of the platform where, in a manner not unlike the little girl from *The Exorcist*, I began to regurgitate everything else I had consumed that evening. At the same time another train pulled up to the station spilling a sea of people out onto the platform, every one of them headed towards me. I wanted to stop regurgitating as much as it was humanly possible for anyone to want anything but I'd started the process and no amount of wishful thinking could stop it. If only my body would respond to my brain's instruction that it really wasn't a good time to eject waste, why doesn't the body work that way? I remained helpless on the side of the platform spewing my guts up into a bush whilst that small army of people hurried past regarding me with disgusted eyes. From out of the crowd I picked out a single sentence as one man said to his friend, "Ooo he's had a good night." If I could have stopped throwing up long enough, I'd have told him in no uncertain terms that I'd had better.

When I turned up for work the following day my manager pulled me aside as soon as I set foot in the door, "Chris, we've got to talk." he said solemnly. I followed him around the side of the bakery. "Where did you disappear to last night? You know we had a meal booked. We couldn't start because we were waiting for you to arrive. I sent Saul and Amy back to the pub to look for you, they searched absolutely everywhere."

"Sorry Alan," I ventured still feeling the worse for wear, "after everyone left, I finished my drink and realised I didn't know exactly where the restaurant was, I must've gone the wrong way." As excuses went it was flimsy by anyone's standards.

"Don't give me that, you know it was next door." I almost laughed but I held it in much better than I held things in the previous night. "You want to watch how much you're drinking Chris." Alan said sternly as he walked off muttering to himself. After a few steps he turned his head back towards me sharply and barked, "You drank too much!" emphasizing his point much more comically than he might have intended.

Christopher Moore

Where's the Four?

Probably the best thing to come out of my time working in the bakery was meeting my best friend Jason, I'm not sure exactly how long it is we've been friends but it's no small amount of years. Jason is a little shorter than me, probably around five foot ten, bald, and as good a guy as you could ever hope to meet. Over the years Jason and I have been through a hell of a lot together, there's more drunken nights out than I can honestly remember and enough stories to fill a second book, probably even a third. He has always been there whenever I've needed him, he was the best man at my wedding and after accidently booking us a double bed in the hotel the night before the Download festival, he we went and explained to the receptionist that we needed tools to fix that bed after the two straight men sleeping together in it had managed to make it collapse. Honestly, we just sat on it.

This particular night out had started out as they often did, in Christchurch Park with a few cans of beer. I was working my way through a crate of Stella and Jason would have had the equivalent of whatever it was he was drinking. It was a pretty hot summer's day and we were enjoying having a laugh and knocking back some cold ones in the sun.

The problem with daytime drinking is there's so much more time for things to go wrong than if you start in the evening, making that invisible line between being a little bit tipsy and completely wasted so much easier to reach. The worst thing is when you do cross that line and you wake up in the morning having no idea what you've said, or what you've done, or even how you made it home, all you can do is hope whatever it was, it wasn't too bad. At least, back then, that was pretty much the extent of your worries, these days, since we all have phones, you have to worry about who you might have called or messaged on top of that. Now, when I wake up after a night out, I check my wallet, my keys and my phone before going back to sleep for as long as my body will allow. I'm getting old, recovery times have increased. Even if you weren't wasted though, it doesn't mean your friends were so well behaved, an unlocked and unattended phone is a dangerous thing indeed. I remember one time when Jason and Peter fell out because Peter had taken his father's phone with him on a night out instead of his own. Jason, not realising it wasn't Peter's phone, had taken full advantage of him leaving it on the table when he went to the bathroom and sent a text that simply read "Suck me off" to all every single contact in the phone. Contacts which would have included all of Peter's father's friends and family not to mention his colleagues at work and even his boss. Peter was not amused and I dare say his father did not see the funny side either. The person who invents an application that will legitimately stop you being able to send drunken messages will make millions. Sometimes I really miss those days before the smartphone, it really was a simpler time.

After we'd consumed all the beer, we had with us we began to make our way out of the park, that invisible drinking line well and truly crossed. As we walked, we came across a game of bowls being played by a group of elderly gentlemen who were relaxing and thoroughly enjoying the quiet tranquility of their surroundings. One of the senior citizens was poised on the green ready to send his wood hurtling towards the jack at the other end of the rink, when a loud noise startled him breaking his concentration. The loud noise in question was Jason's voice that echoed in his ears as he shouted, "Bowls is for gays." at the top of his lungs. Don't worry, I know what you're thinking, you can't just go around shouting "Bowls is for gays." at a bunch of elderly men and their lady friends who are minding their own business, playing the only 'sport' left that they're able to properly perform. They'll be an outcry, a lynch mob, a gaggle of outraged passers-by, and seniors, looking for the source of those horrible words. The culprits will surely be in a lot of trouble. Don't worry. We were behind a bush.

Our sides freshly split from the hilarity of Jason's quick wit we proceeded on our journey, pausing only briefly to climb into a large digger for a photo opportunity. The area was trapped off for safety reasons of course, but I was pretty sure that entering for the purposes of a drunken picture shouldn't be considered a safety hazard, and I was right, mission accomplished. It would've been great if Jason had accidentally put that sucker in gear though. That would have really capped off the day for those seniors on the bowling green, Jason hurtling towards them in a digger screaming, "I told you it was for gays! You wouldn't listen!" as he sends them scattering into the trees.

One of the local Ipswich bars /nightclubs at the time was a place called Pals. We decided to head there after we left the park because Jason had said this girl, he knew was there for a salsa lesson and that was a good enough reason for me. By this time, we were in a very intoxicated state and were probably lucky to even get served but the bar staff, who obviously either hadn't been trained well or couldn't have cared less, poured our beers and pointed us in the direction of the salsa class. To the right of the bar a black curtain hung in the doorway to another room where the lesson was taking place, we walked through the curtain and took our seats as the classes only two spectators.

The class was in full swing already when we arrived and, although it seemed to be going well at first, we hadn't been there long when the atmosphere in the room began to sour. I'm not sure exactly why, but it seemed none of the students, or the instructor, valued our constructive criticism. It was almost as if they knew we didn't have any formal dance training ourselves, still I'm pretty sure Bruce Forsyth wasn't a trained dancer yet he still judged *Strictly Come Dancing*: I've since researched this and it turns out Sir Bruce was a professional dancer.

As Jason and myself did our best to help and advise, and that's what we were doing, helping, not heckling, helping, there was a particularly angry male participant who was aggressively attempting to dance himself closer to where we were seated. The infuriated dancer had said something worrying about wanting to fight us, but for some reason he couldn't just come over and confront us. I have no idea why but, to achieve the desired conflict, he had to get to us while maintaining his salsa. We kept a close eye on the sulky salsa man because, those hips don't lie, he was slowly getting closer. I wondered, had he gotten to us, what exactly he would've done. I'm presuming, as he stuck to the beat so stubbornly, he would have unleashed a bit of Capoeira on us because, if he wasn't and expert in the art of Brazilian dance fighting, I'd have been more than a little disappointed.

The threat of violence lingered in the air but ultimately, he was a salsa dancer not a fighter and he, almost, let it go. I say 'almost' because he did have one other confrontational trick up his sleeve, one other card to play, that of the fabled dance off. I had never been challenged to a dance off before, and indeed have not been since. "Right," the sullen salsa man shouted, "if you think you know so much, let's see if you can do better!" I looked at Jason a little panicked, helpfully he shrugged and took another sip of his beverage. I was on my own. I'd had no time to properly warm up or stretch. I had no routine worked out. I didn't know how to dance. I got to my feet and busted out some appalling out of time and lacklustre dance moves with a drunken man's confidence, I was convinced I'd done pretty well, my opponent had been served. My challenger, who did not agree, audibly scoffed at my efforts, "Huh, that was awful, is that the best you can do?" A smug smile played on his lips and he rotated his hips back towards the centre of the lesson.

I took my seat again and took a sip of my beer, "Better than you, you loser." I laughed, almost falling off my stool. Salsa man was fuming and glared at me incensed, although, despite his visible anger, he decided to take no further action. I had won my first, and only, dance off.

The dance lesson continued and our comments had given way, for the time being, to the enjoyment of our drinks. As we happily drank and talked in the background the lesson progressed. The instructor counted out the beat for the students to help them keep time, "One, two, three," she said rhythmically, "five, six, seven eight." Over and over again she repeated this while we drank, "One, two, three… five, six, seven, eight." Calmly we continued drinking, "One, two, three… five, six, seven, eight."

Jason, who was now sitting quietly holding his beer, wore a perplexed expression on his face, I hadn't thought to ask why. "Hey," he began as if something of great importance had just occurred to him, "where's the four?"

The instructors count continued, "One, two, three… five, six, seven, eight." and slowly I realised Jason was absolutely right, where was the four? This instructor, this so-called professional couldn't even count to eight, and not only was she getting it wrong every single time, she was missing out my favourite number, my lucky number, the number four. The injustice of it was overwhelming. I was furious. I couldn't fathom how this person had gotten through life without the number four. I could not let this travesty slide.

Standing up from my seat I shouted at the top of my voice, "OI, WHERE'S THE FOUR?" All in caps, that's how loud I shouted it. That's how incensed I was by this blatant exclusion of the number four. Still, at a volume vastly exceeding a normal conversational tone of voice, I carried on. I let them know in no uncertain terms exactly what my favourite number was and that I felt very strongly that it should be included every time anyone was to engage in the counting of numbers beyond three. At this point our welcome in the salsa class was unsurprisingly worn out and we were unceremoniously asked to leave. With the threat of security being called to escort us on our way we quickly finished our drinks and hastily made our way to the exit, or at least what we believed was the exit.

We stumbled noisily through our chosen door which closed behind us leaving us, to our surprise, in almost total darkness. There was a door to the left that lead outside but it was locked shut and no amount of rattling the handle was going to get that mother open, which isn't to say we didn't try, we most definitely did. With that door refusing to budge we turned to the only other available option, the stairs. If there's no way out on the ground floor isn't it only logical to go up? With a lack of alternatives, we decided it was worth a shot.

Slowly we climbed the stairs into darkness. Upstairs was pitch black and when you're ever so slightly inebriated and in the dark, finding a light switch isn't an easy task. We felt our way down the corridor, amazed that there didn't seem to be a single bastard light switch on the entire floor, and tried every door we came across. All of them were locked. All of them. For a few minutes more we searched, frantically trying to find something, anything, all we wanted was a way out. We weren't in Alcatraz for God's sake; you'd think there would be some way. In the end, we knew there was but one way out, one means of escape and although the conclusion was obvious, it was one that appealed to neither of us. We had to go back through the salsa class. Back into an area where, just because of the absence of the number four, we were now universally hated.

Hesitantly we opened the door stepping slowly and stealthily back into the classroom, determined that we would slip past unseen. It was a good plan in theory but we were more visible than a squatting sprinter in front of a glass fronted restaurant, instantly every eye in the room was focused on us and, although I was very intoxicated, I still felt the hostility coming from those salsa dancers. I thought, as many of us would, that salsa dancers were a forgiving people, I was wrong, they're not in the slightest, they hold a grudge. It was like being confronted by a very upbeat lynch mob, angry, but loose in the hips. With our heads down we hurried back through the black curtain and out of the correct door to freedom and to seek out a friendlier watering hole. A pub where two men with an opinion to share on the medium of dance, or indeed any other subject they might care to comment on, would be welcomed in with open arms, grateful ears and perhaps even a thought provoking debate if the opinion put forth did not meet with the most popular consensus. These salsa dancers are pure savages.

Flush You Bastard

Up until we travelled to New York in 2001 my family holidays had never been abroad; we went on caravanning holidays in places like Bournemouth which I had always enjoyed as a child. New York was obviously something entirely different from our usual excursions and I was extremely grateful that my parents were taking my sisters and I on this once in a lifetime trip. At the time I don't think I fully appreciated the cost involved in going on such a holiday, my parents must have scrimped and saved for a long time in order to take us.

We were staying in a hotel called The Sheraton which is located on Times Square right in the heart of the city, and from there we went and saw all the usual tourist sights such as The Statue of Liberty, The Empire State Building, The Twin Towers, Central Park, Grand Central Station, WWE (then WWF) New York and Ellis Island. I know WWE New York is long since closed down and possibly not on most people's list of things to do in New York City but for me, as a lifelong wrestling fan, it was somewhere I had to visit, especially since it was located on Times Square and only a few minutes' walk from our hotel.

My favourite place to eat in New York was by far Planet Hollywood, which was also located on Times Square, not only was the food amazing but the portions were huge. I remember seeing a sign on the way in saying to make sure you left room for dessert, despite eating there several times I never managed to order dessert, the portions were that big, and I'm known as someone who can eat. It wasn't only the food there that I enjoyed though because the place was full of props from movies which I loved, an actual proton pack from *Ghostbusters*, the axe from *The Shining* and a full-size ninja turtle from the *Teenage Mutant Ninja Turtles* movie were personal highlights. The first night we were in New York we went to Planet Hollywood; it must have been only a couple of hours after we got off the plane. I had a bad case of aeroplane ear, or ear barotrauma if you prefer the technical term, and I couldn't hear a thing. It was because of this hearing malfunction that I accidently ordered myself an astronomically priced souvenir glass with my five-dollar chocolate milkshake. There, that should be enough of a plug to get a royalty from Schwarzenegger and Stallone.

Even though we were getting to see all these amazing sights and attractions, our trip to New York City did not run smoothly one hundred percent of the time. My father had fallen ill after eating some dodgy noodles from a market stall and, similarly, I had acquired an upset stomach after eating a hotdog purchased on top of the Empire State Building. Unfortunately, these things happen to the best of us and we were determined not to waste our precious time in New York laid up and miserable so we ploughed on and went for a wander in Little Italy, which was a lovely neighbourhood and a popular tourist spot.

After walking around there for some time we were feeling a little peckish, well I say we but it was more my mother and sisters who were unencumbered by illness, so we decided to stop for something to eat. I forget the name of the restaurant we found ourselves in but it was a lovely little pizzeria located on the corner of the street which had large windows showing off the inviting interior. We entered and we were greeted by a smiling server who guided us to a table for five. I sat down at the table and studied the menu, never being one to refuse food I ordered myself a large pizza and excused myself to use the bathroom.

The way I was feeling, if I was going to put any quantity of food into my body then something had to come out first. There was only one toilet in the restaurant and it was unisex. Only one toilet meant, quite obviously, that only one person at a time could use it, so I was lucky it unoccupied and it was also well maintained, on the surface anyway. I hurriedly sat on the throne and loudly unclenched allowing the putrid diarrhea excrement to fall out of me splattering the inside of the bowl like a Jackson Pollock. I quickly executed a courtesy flush before hastily, yet thoroughly, wiping and flushing again to get rid of the dirty sheets of paper. Something was wrong, flush two had not been executed properly at all and instead of swiftly removing the contents of the bowl it made a worrying gurgling sound and just added more water. Understandably panicked I pumped the flush handle, "Come on," I cried, "fucking flush you fucking bastard." I Apologise for my profanity but I think a little colourful language is more than excusable when confronted with a literal brown trousers situation. My concerns grew substantially when I realised the effect my constant yanking of the flush had on my predicament. The lavatory was now full to the brim of water and fecal matter. And it wasn't stopping at the brim, in fact it wasn't stopping at all. As far as I could see I had two choices.

Number One: Plunge my hand into the murky depths and try and free up the blockage.

Number Two: Leave and hope for the best.

By now the water was advancing slowly across the floor towards me, so I did the only sensible thing, I did what any of you would have done in my situation… I ran away. Stepping back out of the bathroom I quickly closed the door behind me and rejoined my family. The food had not yet been served and, as we waited, I anxiously looked back at the toilet door where I could see the water was beginning to seep out from the bathroom and into the dining area. I was really worried at this point. Not only was I unwell but I was sure there would be witnesses who had seen me enter and leave the toilet, fingers could soon be pointed and aspersions cast. How long would it be before someone else needed to go and spotted the advancing tides? How long would it be before someone smelled the dirty water flowing openly under the bathroom door and into the restaurant? I looked back to my family, "Where's dad?" I asked, suddenly noticing his absence.

Now as you'll remember my father hadn't been feeling his best as well. My mother informed me he'd come over a little bit queasy and gone outside for some fresh air. I looked across the room, through the large glass windows to see if I could see where he had gotten to. Moments later I had my answer. My father stood outside the window, bold as brass, trying to get our attention by waving and pointing. We all stared at him and tried to make out what he was trying to say as he mouthed some unknown words and pointed frantically towards the ground. Collectively our gazes followed the direction my father indicated where we saw what it was, he so desperately wanted to highlight to us. It was vomit. A terrifyingly large amount of vomit that ran in large brightly coloured chunks down the lower part of the pizzeria windows and onto the floor. I looked back at the bathroom, the perilous puddle of excrement advanced steadily into the restaurant. I looked back at my father who was still gesturing towards the foul broth that had escaped his body. And then I turned back to my mother, "Shall we leave?" I stated as calmly as I was able. We all got up and, dragging my father away from his window dressing, made a swift exit down the street.

I imagined it would have been but mere minutes after we departed that our waitress would have returned with my family's freshly cooked pizzas only to find that said family were now missing. In confusion she'll have looked around and spotted something on the window, something that doesn't reflect too well on the quality of the food served within the restaurant given its placement on their glass. Following this horror, I imagine there would have been a scream as the sloppy brown waters, still moving ever further forwards, make contact with the customer in closest vicinity to the toilets. I stifled a little chuckle as we moved briskly away.

I really loved New York City. I thought it was an amazing place, and when it came time for us to return to England, I was extremely reluctant to leave. It was only a matter of months after our visit, on September 11th 2001, terrorists flew two planes into the Twin Towers killing thousands of innocent people and shocking the world. I think 9/11 is one of those events where everybody who is old enough to remember, knows exactly where they were when they heard the news. I was at work in the bakery when a colleague mentioned it to me and on completing my shift, I returned home to watch the reports for myself. As somebody who generally avoids watching the news because I find it depressing, I almost didn't want to switch on the television, on this occasion though, I had no choice. I sat for hours watching footage of the incident and listening to the updates of the rescue efforts along with all the speculation about who was responsible and I couldn't believe or begin to process any of it. The fact that anybody could have done such a thing on purpose seemed completely alien to me, I didn't want to acknowledge there were people walking around planning things like that.

As truly tragic and horrible as the events that day were, I also saw a lot of hope in how everyone in the city came together in their time of need to save as many lives as possible. I think it goes to show that no matter how bad things get, or how dark the days, that there will always be good people that are willing to help and even risk their own lives to do so. Those heroes are inspirations and examples to the rest of us. I hope one day I'll get to return to New York again.

Christopher Moore

Cigarettes & Petrol

Although working in the bakery was relatively easy, it wasn't something I was content to do for the rest of my life. I had seen plenty of people around the store who'd been there twenty plus years, that sort of time spent under the artificial lights takes its toll on a person. Next time you take a trip around a supermarket take a look around at the lifers, look at their pale skin and their faraway expressions and ask yourself just how long those poor bastards have been there, ask yourself how long could you be there. I'd go into work every morning and start noticing everything about these people, I wondered where the line was, just how many years does it take before the brain checks out and you slip into autopilot? Were they even still human? How long before I was just like them? One thing was for sure, I didn't want to stick around and find out.

Eventually I found myself another job and I was ecstatic to finally be working in graphic design. At long last I was showing that careers advisor at school who told me I could never be a designer that I most definitely could, never let anyone tell you that you can't do anything. Now if only I could have found that smug little peacock to even up the score there, then I'd have known I was really on my way up. I was working for a company called Pilkington Design & Print who handled website design & build and retail solutions. I started at the bottom building displays and driving around the country to install them, before later working as a designer, then a programmer and then eventually running their large format print division. I liked working there and always did everything I could to succeed and advance in the company, if the company hadn't eventually folded, I doubt I would ever have left.

During my early career with Pilkington Design & Print I was doing a lot of driving, but when I started, I wasn't the most experienced driver, not by a long shot. In fact, someone else in the company had told me he wasn't permitted to drive any hire vehicles because he didn't have enough experience, nobody ever asked how long I'd been driving or how much experience I had. That person I worked with who wasn't allowed behind the wheel, he was significantly more experienced than I was, next to him I was a novice. I may as well have had stabilizers on my car, like the ones you might find on a child's bike, and my driving license may as well have been written in crayon, that's how inexperienced I was. I learnt to drive in, and owned a Nissan Micra and suddenly I was being asked to drive long wheelbase transit vans all over the country, it was a recipe for disaster. My problems weren't limited to experience though, I was also absolutely useless with directions, this was quite a big problem because we had no satellite navigation, just old school maps and printouts which I had to try and read while driving, needless to say, I frequently got lost. On one occasion I went into a shop to ask directions to the place I was looking for, much to the amusement of the member of staff I asked, who took great pleasure in informing me that the place I was unable to locate without his assistance was located next door, obscured from sight by a large hedge. That flipping hedge made me look like a right tit.

There were multiple times during my adventures on the road that I was almost killed, if you're on the road long enough you're bound to have a few close calls. Almost dying is alright though, I can handle almost dying, what I can't handle is being stuck behind the wheel while desperate for the toilet, that's agony. Many's the time I've found myself hurtling down the motorway at seventy miles an hour carrying a full bladder, my legs jiggling impatiently, a bead of sweat on my brow, then at long last I'd see that all important sign that I'd been waiting for that would finally tell me where the services are, only to find that they're fifty bloody miles away. Even though I travelled all over the country for the company the two main incidents I had both occurred within a few miles of the office, the first less than a minutes' drive away. Neither involved wetting myself, although that might have been preferable.

It'd been a long day at work and I'd been out driving all day in a brand-new hire car. I'd arrived back at the office a few hours behind schedule, thanks to the traffic, and was desperate to get home as soon as possible because I was back out on the road first thing the next morning. It was late, it was dark and I was tired but I decided to fill the car up that night to get a head start on the morning. I pulled in to Tesco petrol station at Martlesham Heath and opened the glove box of the car, I was looking for a manual because I had no idea what sort of fuel the car took, sadly the glove box was empty, except for a dusty travel sweet that looked like it had seen better days, the lone survivor of some long forgotten journey, I closed the glove box and continued the search. I looked everywhere for some sort of indication of fuel type but, as far as I could see, there wasn't one. It was not an ideal situation, not by any means, but I didn't think it was the end of the world because I was pretty sure I'd heard somewhere that the wrong nozzle wouldn't fit into a car which took another sort of fuel, it was like putting a square peg into a round hole, and this reassured me enough to at least attempt a refuel. The car looked like it was probably an unleaded car to me so I reached for the green pump, it fit like a glove and so I proceeded to fill the tank. I stood on the forecourt watching the numbers on the gauge rise until eventually the car was full, I removed the pump and went to close the filler cap. It was just as I was closing the cover a little bit of light caught the metal inside illuminating out of the darkness a tiny sticker that just read 'DIESEL'.

I gasped as I realised what I'd done. This was a big mistake, and I mean big, as mistakes go this was an absolute whopper. For a minute I just stood there, I honestly considered just walking away, leaving the car at Tesco and heading back to the bakery where I worked previously to see if I could have my old job back. I didn't do that but with my available options it was definitely feeling like a contender. I felt sick to my stomach knowing that my only course of action was to return to the office, try and catch my boss before he left and own up. I paid for the fuel and got back in the car. I knew it shouldn't be driven with the wrong fuel in the tank but I was pretty sure I could limp it around the corner to the office.

My boss, Jack, was a really good guy most of the time and we got on very well, but understandably he was annoyed about this and I was mortified about having been so foolish. Jack didn't want to call the garage to tell them what I'd done as he was afraid there would be a substantial cost involved so he instead informed me that he would bring a hose in the following morning first thing, and I would be syphoning the tank.

I had never syphoned a tank of petrol before and I'll be completely honest, the idea did not appeal to me. Basically, what it involved was placing a hose into the petrol tank and sucking on it until the petrol started coming out, which would then be collected in a container. I wasn't happy but I started sucking. Don't do the crime if you can't do the time as they say, and I imagine the sequence of events would be pretty much the same for a hardened criminal as it was for me, i.e., commit a crime, go to prison, start sucking and finally, take a shot in the mouth. When that first mouthful of unleaded hit the back of my throat I gagged and I was very nearly sick. Petrol does not taste as good as you might imagine. As I spat the liquid out into the bucket, I noticed I had an audience of co-workers, this made the process all the more humiliating and the feeling of being watched only added to my prison time comparisons. Although I'd achieved a couple of good mouthfuls of petrol, that was all I was able to get from the tank so before long I called it quits and had to phone the hire company so I was able to get back out on the road. The worst thing about the whole episode, for me, was that I smoked, how long do you wait after having a mouth full of petrol before you're sure it's safe to light a cigarette again? I was understandably apprehensive, I thought of the scene in *Zoolander* where the models have a petrol fight on the forecourt before blowing themselves up with a cigarette... and I left it fifteen minutes.

The other incident I had was probably worse, it was more dangerous certainly and, in retrospect, I was lucky to escape without a scratch on me. Something I did achieve in the process of nearly dying though, was that for the first and only time in my life I made the news! Well I say the news, I mean the traffic report... for Ipswich... on local radio. It's close enough.

I was in a large wheelbase transit heading back to Martlesham Heath from Devon where I'd been installing a display in their local Homebase store. Homebase is a chain of home and garden superstores found throughout the country. I went to all the Homebases. You name a Homebase store and, if it's not been opened in the last twenty years or so, then I've been in it. I got to see all the Homebases and, this might surprise you if you were thinking of going further afield in search of a more exotic Homebase, they're all pretty similar.

I had phoned the office ahead to tell them when I estimated I'd arrive back at the office as my colleague Patrick was waiting to use the van. I'd stayed overnight in Devon so I was going to be back in plenty of time before the end of the working day, in fact I was going to be back early enough to have a sneaky break in a nearby car park before I pulled back into the office. I was on the home stretch, heading down the A12 towards Felixstowe and turning off onto the A14 heading to Martlesham, when things went slightly wrong.

It turns out that just because you can take a corner at forty-five miles an hour in a Nissan Micra, that doesn't necessarily mean the rule applies for all vehicles. I turned left, thundering around the corner with the stereo on full blast, when I noticed the backend felt funny, it was beginning to tip over. Instinctively and frantically I turned the wheel back in the opposite direction to counteract the fall and land the back wheel back on the tarmac, but in doing so the momentum made the wheel on the opposite side take off and the van began to tip that way instead. The more I tried to correct it the more momentum built up in a terrifying rocking motion until, in a matter of moments, the back end of the transit was airborne and landing with a crash on top of the central reservation on the motorway. As the van ground to a halt, hung up on the metal crash barrier, I took a deep breath and looked down and my hands, they were shaking. Not wanting to hang around just in case another motorist came around the corner and ran into the back of me, I flicked the hazards on, jumped out and ran to the hard shoulder. On the other side of the motorway another car had skidded to a halt in the layby and the driver ran over to meet me on my side of the road, "Holy shit dude that was awesome!" he said, thrilled to bits with what he'd just seen, "Are you ok? You really took off there."

"Yeah I'm alright." I said feeling in my pocket for my cigarettes which, to my dismay, I realised I'd left in the van. After a quick jog over the carriageway to retrieve them, and a smoke to calm my nerves, I phoned the office and asked for Patrick. "Hello mate, I've got some good news and some bad news. The good news is I'm just down the road... but... the bad news is I've crashed the van and I need you to send recovery out." I stood next to that van for three long hours waiting for it to be taken off the barrier along with the police who closed off a lane of the motorway until the recovery services arrived.

Standing beside the road and waiting for hours on end is bad enough but combine that with other motorists slowing down to offer their comments as they pass by and you've got a real bastard of an afternoon to contend with. "Nice parking mate." was a witty jape I must have heard at least twenty times. Everybody's a comedian. There was an enjoyable moment, however, when one of those passing motorists stopped to take himself a little picture of the accident and was seen in this endeavour by one of the policemen. Now up until this point the police hadn't said anything to any of the motorists who slowed down to comment, for some reason this had been allowed no questions asked, but it turns out if you go for the souvenir photo that's when the police spring into action.

"Hey you!" the policemen yelled angrily as he approached the rear of the car, "What do you think you're doing taking pictures?" The driver of the car glanced back behind him, and seeing the approaching officer, decided his best course of action was certainly not to stick around for a scolding, the best thing he could do was drive. With a loud screeching of tires, the man accelerated away down the road, at which point the policeman gave chase… on foot. It was like watching Robert Patrick's T-1000 running after John Connor in *Terminator 2: Judgement Day*, I don't know how that policeman thought he was going to catch the car but I'll give him this, he gave it a bloody good try.

Christopher Moore

Stabbed

My days driving around the country for Pilkington Design & Print were over. I was still with the company but after crashing a van and putting the wrong fuel into a car I'd gotten much too expensive to insure; I can't imagine why. It worked out for the best though, because not being on the road allowed me to move properly into graphic design, and that was exactly where I wanted to be, although I still helped out a fair amount in the retail side of the business as well where I was building displays instead of driving them around.

One such display which we were producing in large quantities was designed to sell a range of landline telephones. Each display consisted of around fifteen phones, each one of those was screwed onto a red plastic board containing an information graphic on the right hand side and the phone on the left, then each board was mounted three wide and five deep on a large MDF backboard, and then the whole thing was encased in Perspex. The finished product was around a metre wide by a metre and a half high. We had been making a bunch of them simultaneously and had the MDF panels balanced on two sawhorses each, up and down the warehouse. I was busy preparing to paint the edges of the MDF panels white and, using a screwdriver, I levered the lid off of the paint can and, once opened, placed it on the end of one of the MDF panels whilst I fetched the paint rollers and trays.

I was never a fan of painting because I've always hated getting messy, so it was very reluctantly I agreed to any job involving painting anything. Still during my time at Pilkington Design & Print, I painted not only the displays but almost the entire interior of the building as well as the fence that surrounded the car park. I certainly paid my dues before I found success in that place.

Having acquired the brushes I needed I headed back to the warehouse where I'd left the open can of paint waiting, it was a short walk and you'd have been forgiven for assuming there was nothing that could go wrong in the ten to fifteen seconds it took me to complete the journey, regrettably though, this was not the case. I walked briskly and with purpose, keen to get the painting over and done with so I could move onto a more interesting task, when I caught my left foot on one of the sawhorses. I half turned in surprise as I tripped and began to fall. Nobody ever expects to be tripped and to fall down that's why whenever we do suffer a slight stumble, like stepping off an unexpected kerb, we feel rather foolish no matter how minor it may be. If we do have a more major fall, one where we're likely to end up hitting the ground, we will probably all react the same way and reach out instinctively for anything to grab hold of that may break said fall. That's exactly what I did. It just so happened that the nearest thing for me to grab hold of was an MDF panel, and it also just so happened that, that particular MDF panel was the same one that I'd used to rest my can of white emulsion paint.

I looked up, the brand-new can of paint had been catapulted skyward from the opposite side of the MDF panel and now soared above me like a fat, metallic bird. I could feel my jaw drop as I watched it, the split second it had taken for this to happen seemed to last for a lifetime but I knew that what had gone up must, inevitably, come down, and I was powerless to stop it. If you've never seen the kind of mess that is created by launching a full can of white paint across a room then you'll have to trust me when I say it's quite a thing to behold. Paint covered absolutely everything from the ceiling tiles to the carpet and it was going to take more than a damp cloth and some kitchen towel to clean it up, that was for sure. My heart sank as I surveyed the scene before me, it looked like a thousand pigeons had flown through the building, carpet bombing the place as they went… or maybe even… a thousand peacocks. A picture of my brightly coloured nemesis flashed before my eyes, further tormenting me in my darkest hour… or lightest hour even, given the colour of the paint. I closed my eyes for a second to calm myself down, maybe things weren't as bad as I thought. I opened my eyes again, a large clump of paint oozed down from the ceiling and landed with a loud, yet strangely satisfying, splat onto one of the new displays, which was ruined along with most of the others, nope, it was pretty bad. I bit the bullet and told my boss what had happened, I thought it better than waiting until he saw it for himself, although neither option was going to be easy. Luckily my boss wasn't too angry, at least not outwardly, he simply said, "Clean it up." To be honest that was a fate much worse than any other punishment I can imagine.

A few years later, when the company invested in large format printers, I'd helped install them and had been one of only a handful of people trained in their operation. The printers were based in a huge room upstairs that nobody else went in, I'd always fancied my own office so I moved my computer up there without even talking to my employers, making the executive decision myself that I would run the department. It was true, in doing so I'd be on my own nearly all day everyday but I didn't mind in the slightest, plus, if I got too lonely I knew I could always print myself out some new friends, that was the kind of power I wielded in my new role.

Sometime later the building was reshuffled and my print room was moved downstairs into a new office and, with a high demand for my services, I received an additional member of staff in the form of a little gothic apprentice called Norman. If you can picture in your head a small Noel Fielding with acne then you've got a pretty good image in your head of Norm. As much as I liked being alone it was good to have someone in my office every day that I could have a laugh with again, I'd almost forgotten how much fun work could be with company. I liked to play the occasional prank on Norm to keep him on his toes, if he left the room he'd often come back to find his desktop wallpaper had been changed to a picture of a homosexual celebrity, usually Christopher Biggins, because I'd come across a really funny picture of him laying naked on the floor in black and white. Maybe "come across" was a poor choice of words. It was always funny when someone else saw the image before he could change it back, I think a lot of members of staff probably had some serious questions about Norman.

I spent a large amount of my working life with a scalpel in my hand, probably even more so than a surgeon and I would wager I was just as skilled. In a job where freehand cutting was essential, I had a good eye and a steady hand. I was the best. Even though I was very good with a scalpel, that does not mean I never had any accidents, in fact, quite the opposite, I worked very long hours and the occasional cut from tiredness alone, was inevitable. Looking at my hands now, I can still see the scars from some particularly nasty slips but the worst one I had by far did not even graze a finger and left a scar somewhere else entirely… no… not there.

I'd been spending the day cutting out various graphics with large straight edge cutter we were able to use on anything with… well, with a straight edge. Despite being several metres in length the cutter wasn't big enough for every job and in this particular instance I was left with some waste either side of the cut I'd just made which needed to be removed before I could proceed and cut the next edge. Ordinarily I'd have done this in a sensible manner but I had a tight deadline to meet so I decided to quickly slice off the excess on the panel with a scalpel, it wasn't a very safe way to proceed but it was fast. I cut carelessly towards myself and slipped. Suddenly the blade was traveling at great velocity towards my body.

At first, I felt nothing, not even the slightest pinch, but as I looked down at the cold metal handle of the scalpel, I knew that I should definitely have felt something, given that the inch-long blade was now imbedded in my stomach. Even so, my first thought and primary concern was for my t-shirt more than it was my own wellbeing, you see I was wearing my favourite Ginger Wildheart t-shirt from his acoustic 2008 tour, this t-shirt held special significance to me as I'd purchased it after I was able to get on stage with Ginger himself, at a bar called The Water Rats in London, and play percussion on several songs. Now, as I looked down at the t-shirt, I could see it had a hole in it where the scalpel had broken through on its way to my stomach, it was ruined. After I'd spent two or three long seconds mourning my t-shirt, the pain finally hit me and my t-shirt fast became the secondary concern it should have been from the start.

"Urgh, argh, shit, uh, fuck." I swore and groaned and groaned and swore until, eventually, Norman began to become aware that something was wrong. He turned his head away from his computer to look towards where I stood partially hidden from his sight by both a bench and a laminator.

"Hey mate, are you alright?" Norman enquired, much too casually for the seriousness of the situation. I looked down at the shiny metal handle that protruded from my belly like a Cyberman's penis and shook my head.

"Nope, no, I'm not alright," I said through gritted teeth, "I've just stabbed myself!"

Norman looked at me and smirked, "Of course you have," he replied, running a hand through his greasy, black, gothic hair, "very funny." I looked at him slightly annoyed, I couldn't be too cross with him as I was basically like the boy who cried wolf at this point with all my pranks, so rather than waste my breath trying to convince him I needed help I instead stepped out from behind the bench and let him see for himself.

The smirk vanished from Norman's face in a split second and, I'd say he went as white as a sheet, but, being a Goth, it was hard to tell. With a sense of urgency, I didn't see from him often, Norman sprang into action, "I'll go and get help." he cried with a tremble in his voice. As I watched him leave my office to get a member of staff more qualified to deal with a stab wound, I decided that it was time I removed the blade.

"Alright, you can do this," I said to myself in an effort to psych myself up, "on three." I took a deep breath and got a hold of the handle.

"One." My stomach throbbed in pain, I thought about how careless I'd been and vowed to be more cautious when handling knives in the future.

"Two." I was grateful that the blade, if it had to end up in my body, ended up where it did. I considered the consequences of impact a few inches south, I could have become a DIY Jew or, even worse, a eunuch. I felt my balls retreat inside my body at the thought of what might have happened.

"Three." Swiftly I pulled the scalpel free like King Arthur pulling the sword from the stone, except with more blood. My hand was visibly shaking as I held the freshly removed scalpel, I looked at it and let it fall through my fingers to the floor as I slumped down to a seated position against the benches holding my freshly probed belly like a cowboy who'd taken a gunshot wound.

Seconds later Norman returned with my boss Jack, "You alright Chris? Norm says you've hurt yourself."

I looked up at the pair of them stood above me, my hand clamped over the wound and my t-shirt sticky with blood. "Yeah. Just a little stab wound, give me a minute or two and I'll be fine." I don't know why I felt the need to play it down but that's what I did.

"Are you sure? You might need stitches…" Jack seemed genuinely concerned, as he probably should have been with an employee potentially bleeding out on the floor in front of him.

"Nope, I'll be fine." I insisted, still through gritted teeth, "We'll just tape it up and I'll be good to go." I moved my hand to look at the wound, although deep and unpleasant to look at it wasn't wide and I figured a good piece of gaffa tape would hold it, so I washed it out, got some tape and stuck it back together before hobbling outside the building for a couple of cigarettes to take the edge off before returning to work.

My stomach was sore for a week or two after that but I carried on as if nothing had happened, I know I really should have gone to the hospital but at the time I was more than a little over conscientious when it came to my responsibilities at work and I never liked to let anybody down. These days, given the experiences I've had since then with work related stress and mental health, I'd view things more than a little differently.

Christopher Moore

Cardigan

It had been a long day at work and I'd spent all afternoon waiting for Katie to come in and ask one simple question. That's all I wanted, that's all I craved with the entirety of my being just one simple question. As the seconds ticked towards five o'clock, I smiled to myself like a villain in a bad movie and looked forward to the inevitable.

Katie had been employed by Pilkington Design & Print as a photographer, she was extremely talented but, because there wasn't nearly enough photography work to justify employing a photographer full time, she spent a fair amount of her days assisting me. I never had any objection to having Katie work with me, she was a very attractive girl with dark hair and pretty brown eyes, I was engaged to Jadie at this time but if I'd been single, I have no doubt she'd have been turning me down every single day. Still the two of us got on like a house on fire, so any day we worked together was a fun day.

I often worked hours outside of the normal nine to five, sometimes I was in early, sometimes I stayed late, sometimes both and sometimes I never made it home at all working in excess of twenty-four hours on multiple occasions, it all depended on the job and the deadline. This particular morning, I had come in early and Katie had agreed to do so as well to give us a head start on the day before my apprentice Norman made it into the office.

I look back on those days and regret how much of myself I gave to my work, I never wanted to put in so many hours but I felt it was my responsibility to do so. No matter what it is you do, at the end of the day, a job is a job, family and friends should always come first. Nobody gets to the end of their life and wishes they'd spent more time in the office.

Katie came in, said hello and smiled at me making me briefly forget how tired I was from the early start and how mundane the rest of my day would likely be. Before she joined me at my workbench Katie took off her grey cardigan which she placed neatly on my desk, I instructed her on what needed to be done and we got to work. A little while later Norman arrived and Katie returned to the office next door to carry on with her other tasks for that day saying that if she had any free time, she would return to help out some more later on. Norman placed his dirty looking hoodie and jacket on the back of his chair just like he always did and set about helping me where Katie had left off. It was then that I had a silly little idea, I would bide my time and while Norm wasn't paying attention, I would place Katie's cardigan underneath his hoodie. Yes, it wasn't the greatest practical joke in the world but I expected to get a little laugh from his reaction in finding this unexpected garment with his clothes, anything I hadn't already tried before to make the day go by that little bit faster couldn't be a bad idea. I had to be careful not to be spotted, Norman was still on high alert from when I changed the surname on his email signature slightly to read, Norman Bumder. He'd sent several internal emails before that one was pointed out to him.

When it got to lunch time, Norman picked up all the garments on the back of his chair ready to go to Tesco's and grab some lunch, but as he went to put his arm into his sleeve he stopped in confusion. "Eh, what's this?" he said looking at the cardigan, then at me and back again at the narrower than usual sleeve he was faced with.

"What's what mate?" I asked casually from my workbench. I wanted to appear to pay as little attention as possible to his predicament but I glanced up slyly as I finished cutting out the item I was working on. Two more minutes work then I'd join Norman for the walk to Tesco.

Norman was extremely confused, "This cardigan, why's this cardigan here?" his hand hovered by the arm hole as if an evil force, or perhaps some small rodent, lurked unseen in the synthetic fibres of the sleeve keeping him from placing his hand inside.

I glanced up, "I have no idea, isn't it yours?" I asked casually. I played my hand well, casting a seed of doubt into Norman's mind. Now it was time to nurture that seed, I was breaking out my watering can and watching that mother sprout.

"No, of course it's not. I guess… it must be… my sisters?" he stood there very unsure of himself pausing as he spoke, trying as hard as he could to make sense of its random appearance under his own clothing. "Did I… did I wear this all the way here? I must have picked it up off the banister… with… my… hoodie… did I?" Norman looked up at me as if he wanted confirmation that his theory was sound and, as helpful as ever, I made every effort to put his mind at ease.

"Sounds like you must have mate. You better take it home to her I suppose." I picked up my own coat and started to put it on. The seed was definitely growing, a touch more water perhaps.

"Yeah I better... I better had. I'll put it in my rucksack and take it, home, shall I?" Once again Norman looked to me for approval.

"If it's your sister's cardigan I would. Unless you want to keep it here." With that Norman opened his bag and placed the cardigan inside. I smiled smugly to myself, my little seed of doubt had only grown into a mother flipping beanstalk and I was off with Jack to the land above the clouds. I didn't dare dream things would go this way but I was so happy they had. We left for lunch, and when we returned all I had left to do was wait.

It was ten to five and with the working day nearing completion everyone's thoughts turned to home time. I was finishing off the last few things that needed cutting out at the workbench near the door to the design studio, which was where Katie was working, and Norman sat at his computer getting ready to switch everything off. I looked up and smiled as Katie walked into my office, "Hey there, are you alright?"

Katie smiled sweetly, "I'm good thank you. Sorry I didn't make it back in to help but it's been a nightmare in there today. I'm just looking for my grey cardigan, I think I might have left it here this morning, have you seen it?"

Norman's ears suddenly pricked up and his head shot around to face me, the dots connected in his mind straight away and a look of sheer panic appeared on his face. "Hmm," I said slowly and thoughtfully looking towards Norm, who stared back at me frantically shaking his head knowing full well what I was going to say and wishing he could make me stop, "Norman…" I smiled at him and continued, "didn't I see you putting a grey cardigan in your bag earlier?"

Katie turned and looked at Norman who broke out in a nervous sweat no sooner had the question been asked. "What?" he stammered in reply. I was like a shark smelling blood in the water.

"That erm... that grey cardigan, you took that didn't you? It's in your bag?" I had stitched him right up and he knew it. There was nothing he could say to make it look any less like he'd taken the first opportunity he had and stolen Katie's clothing, and what purpose could a young man have for perpetrating such a crime? Only one sprang to mind.

Norman fumbled around urgently in his bag and produced the cardigan from within, "I'm really sorry." he mumbled apologetically holding it out to her, "I'm really sorry."

"Norman. This might seem like a stupid question but what is my cardigan doing in your bag?" Katie inquired with a genuinely worried expression on her face. I'd love to have known the thoughts that went through Katie's mind as she took the cardigan back. As I mentioned previously, I could only think of one explanation that would occur to me in her shoes and that was that Norman had to be some sort of masturbating cardigan sniffer. I was sure Katie must have arrived at a similar conclusion.

"I thought it was my sisters." Norman said feebly, "I'm so sorry." I felt sorry for Norm, just not sorry enough to stop turning the screws. I knew I could make things right later but, in that moment, I needed to add that sweet, sweet cherry on the delicious fudge sundae that was this heavenly moment.

"Norman," I said scornfully, "you can't just go around taking ladies clothing, that's just not the sort of thing you can go around doing, especially not in the office." I tutted in disappointment at my perverted apprentice who had turned a crimson shade of red.

Katie eyed the pair of us suspiciously before once again addressing Norman, "Don't do anything like that again. It's very weird." and with that she turned around and walked back to the design studio, no sooner had she gone I burst into uncontrollable fits of laughter.

"You bastard!" said Norman, "You knew that was her cardigan the whole time." he said, his embarrassment turning to anger like the flick of a switch.

Still laughing I responded, "Of course I did. Who do you think put it on your chair in the first place?" Norman's eyes widened, obviously he hadn't realised the full extent of my involvement and merely thought he'd placed his jacket on top of her cardigan without noticing first thing that morning.

"You absolute bastard!" he squeaked; his voice having gone up a full octave. I laughed so much I honestly thought I was going to throw up.

I later explained to Katie what had happened because, well, I'm not a complete shit, and Norman was taken off the Pilkington Design & Print sex offenders register.

Christopher Moore

Moist

    As a parent I would have to say the best thing about having a child is the unconditional love that exists between you, from the moment my daughter Faith was born I never wanted to be away from her for a moment in the rest of my life. Every second I was able to, I spent it with Faith, most parents might have a few nights away for break at some point in their child's first few years but I never did, I never wanted it. The first time I left her overnight was when I married her mother Jadie and we went on our honeymoon, Faith was four years old at the time and I didn't want to leave her then. I spent months trying to convince Jadie that we should take her with us and I missed her every second we were gone.

The year before I married Jadie in the run up to Christmas 2009 we decided to take Faith to the cinema to see the latest version of *A Christmas Carol* which starred Jim Carrey. Faith was three and it was her first trip to the cinema. I was excited to take her because she'd never experienced a film on the big screen before and I loved seeing her reactions whenever she was introduced to something new. We took our seats in the cinema, Jadie and myself bookending our daughters, Christina next to Jadie and Faith next to me, and we proceeded to watch the film. At first Faith watched the screen wide eyed, her face full of wonder as she became immersed in the world in front of her, it seemed this was going to be a great experience for her, that was until the ghosts came.

The ghosts of Christmas Past, Present and Future were all a cause of concern for Faith, she was only three after all, and as soon as the first appeared Faith hurriedly moved from her seat to sit on my lap where she felt safer. I was happy Faith was sat with me and I reassured everything was alright and I gave her plenty of cuddles. Next arrived the Ghost of Christmas Present, who was basically an obese gentleman, and fortunately Faith was fine watching him show Scrooge how Bob Cratchit's family were living in poverty. All too soon it was time for the third ghost, the Ghost of Christmas Future, and the atmosphere became a touch more foreboding than it had been previously. I reassured Faith, who was still sat on my lap, that there was nothing to be afraid of but as the Ghost of Christmas Future appeared on the screen, I felt Faith's fear, which was highlighted by a strangely warm sensation in my loins. I sat motionless as the feeling spread, expanding slowly around my groin area. I looked suspiciously at Faith who looked back at me with a worried look in her eyes.

On second thoughts maybe *A Christmas Carol*, despite being rated PG, could in fact be considered a touch on the scary side. Faith had obviously thought so the second she had seen the Ghost of Christmas Future, at least I presume that's what caused to empty her bladder onto my lap, the only other option being because she thought it was a funny thing to do and knowing Faith it was impossible to rule that out entirely. I let out a long sigh and lifted Faith up just enough to look at the large wet patch on my lap, "Yup... it looks like I've pissed myself." I said quietly to myself before placing her back down on my sodden jeans. It didn't matter how much I wanted to see the end of the film, I couldn't sit there and happily watch while both Faith and myself marinated in her urine, it was not a comfortable feeling to endure and I imagined it would only get worse as the pee began to cool. As discreetly as humanly possible, I leant over the seats and told Jadie I would leave her and Christina to watch the end of the film, but, being covered in peeps, Faith and I would be going home to get cleaned up. Now my only problem was how to leave the cinema and get to my car with some small shred of dignity, because walking out of there with a giant wet stain on the front of my trousers would definitely raise the eyebrows of anyone who saw me. I picked my daughter up and headed for the exit.

I could only think of one way to walk out without anyone seeing my front and that was to hold my little girl in front of me like a human shield and act natural. So that's what I did, I faced her forwards, picked her up under the arms and held her out in front of me. The lobby was crowded and I had never felt more self-conscious, it felt as though every pair of eyes in the room was focused on us, I held Faith up, put my head down and legged it. We moved through the lobby at speed as I told Faith, in a hushed tone under my breath, that perhaps peeing on her daddy wasn't the best thing to and perhaps she should have mentioned she needed the bathroom. It's ok Faith, we all have our moments, and at three years old you're allowed to pee on someone every once in a while. As we stepped outside and the cold winter air hit my soaking wet trousers, I instantly became more uncomfortable. The feeling of wetting yourself is bad but to be soaking in someone else's urine, well that's a hundred times worse. I was very glad to get home and get cleaned up, even if it did take me an hour or two to see the funny side.

The next time we went to the cinema I was more wary of the dangers small children posed to the overall theatrical experience but I hoped, having had the experience once, the chances of anything similar happening again were very slim indeed. Over the following years I relaxed, my daughter got older and, knowing she had gained full control over her bladder, I let my guard down, I felt safe. It was another seven years before I left the cinema covered in someone else's urine again.

It was just after Christmas 2016 and I was taking Faith to see the film *Monster Trucks*, which was about a teenager who had a monster living in his truck, obviously. We'd booked our seats and arrived at the cinema; we weren't excited about the film particularly but it was always great to spend time with my baby. Faith and I took our seats in screen two and waited for the trailers to start but as we waited, I noticed something didn't feel right and, not only that, there was an unpleasant smell in the area, a smell not unlike a toilet. It must have been in the performance of the film immediately before ours that a child, or an incontinent senior, had been sitting in my seat, and that unseen seat assassin, that bastard upholstery soaker, had drenched my seat, the one where I was expected to rest my bottom for the next two hours, in urine. Anyway, after a few minutes sat in that discharge-soaked chair, the moisture had saturated my jeans and the moment it reached my skin I suddenly became very aware where the toilet smell I'd been puzzling over originated from, of course, it had to be my seat. I shot up like a bullet letting Faith know instantly what had happened, "Someone's pissed in this chair!" I screamed in panic twisting around frantically to look at my moist posterior. Faith, as helpful as ever, burst out into fits of laughter.

"Sit down dad, you have to stay in your seat." she said between giggles. I was furious beyond all reason but not with the chair soaker, with the cinema. I was incensed that I'd paid to sit in a piss-soaked seat, even though without the parent (or carer) of the child (or senior) that did it reporting what had happened, it would probably have been next to impossible for anyone to spot. I didn't care about that; I wasn't thinking clearly now my bum had been unjustly moistened by the juices of some mystery assailant.

"Wait here Faith, I'm going to go and complain." I said angrily storming out. I walked up to the lady who scanned my ticket on the way in and said, "Excuse me but I'm in screen two and the seat that I've paid for is soaked in urine, which I've just sat in!" I swivelled around angrily to show her my backside, which I pointed down at and wiggled a touch, like a physical exclamation point! How she kept a straight face I'll never know.

"Oh my god I'm really sorry sir, what's your seat number?" she said very apologetically. I gave her the number and was slightly calmed by the fact the lady seemed genuinely interested in helping me. "I'll make sure we get that cleaned as soon as the current performance ends." It sounded like a reasonable enough solution were I not supposed to be in that seat for the duration of the current performance.

"Well I'm moving seats. I'm not sitting in that for two hours." I said sternly, as if that had been what the woman expected of me, then I turned and stormed off to the bathroom to soak up the worst of the pee with some toilet paper and a quick blast of the hand dryer.

When I arrived back at the screen Faith was still laughing and tried to insist that I had to retake my original seat. Even if I mention the incident to her today, she still finds it hilariously funny.

Thanks Faith.

Wet

     I love the sea. I like the calming sound of the waves, I like the cool blue water, I could happily sit on the beach for hours on end just watching the ocean and enjoying the tranquility of those sort of surroundings. I love watching the sea just as much when there's a storm as I do when it's calm, there's nothing like a good storm and seeing the waves swell and crash onto the beach is an amazing sight that I could never tire of. The other thing I find fascinating about the ocean is the shear amount of life there is unseen below the surface, it's because of that I think that as much as I love the sea, I prefer to stay out of it as a general rule. I was a born land mammal and, as much as the water might appeal, I'm out of my element whenever I enter the sea which, I'm all too aware, makes me easy prey for whatever creatures might be waiting in the depths below.

     When my ex-wife Jadie and I went our honeymoon to Turkey in 2010, it was so hot it seemed the only place to get some respite from the heat, was in the water. Before we departed on the trip, I did my research and, because I knew there shouldn't have been anything much to worry about in the Turkish sea, I decided to cool off in there every day. I think that when you're in the sea, no matter what country you are in, you can never consider yourself one hundred percent safe, because the ocean is so vast there's a possibility that anything can pretty much show up anywhere so, despite all reassurances to the contrary, I always had one eye open.

As I lay floating in the water, looking out to sea, I noticed a line of rope in the distance that stretched from left to right as far as I could see. I mentioned the rope to Jadie who told me it was a net that reached the sea floor and kept the beach free of anything dangerous that might swim in. The idea of this huge net captivated me, it seemed like an amazing safety precaution that should have been in use on beaches across the world, although, I did wonder how they prevented the various sea creatures out there from getting tangled in the rope and dying, surely there couldn't be a massive net out there full of dead fish could there? The idea didn't bear thinking about. I decided I had to see this fantastic net for myself and so I convinced Jadie to swim out there with me to have a look.

The net was a fair way from shore, much further than I would have considered going if there wasn't that gigantic net keeping me safe. It took probably around twenty minutes for us both to swim to the net but the ocean was calm and it wasn't a particularly difficult swim, that said it was tiring and by the time we drew close we were both in need of a breather. I made it there first and grabbed hold of the top of the net with my left hand, triumphantly I lifted it out of the water only to find that it wasn't a net at all, it was only a rope, a marker to tell swimmers not to venture out any further. Without the safety net I suddenly felt very conscious of how far away from shore we were and then, when I felt something brush past my foot that may or may not have been imaginary, I completely panicked. It's not something I'm proud of but you have to understand that I was ninety nine percent sure I was about to be eaten. I spun around in the water frantically looking for the shark, and I was sure it was a shark, that had grazed my skin moments earlier. Jadie said I should calm down and we'd swim back, which was all well and good but the shark wasn't after her now was it. I continued to spin trying to locate the shark while looking, to anyone who might have seen, like I'd been caught in some kind of localized whirlpool, and then I felt it, in my left leg out of the blue, sheer agony.

"Agh," I screamed, momentarily disappearing under the water as Jadie swam to reach me. I resurfaced in front of her, spitting out salt water as I struggled to keep my head above the surface but it was no use, I was sinking. My leg was in blinding pain but it was not shark or squid or indeed any kind of aquatic life that seeked to take me under, in my panic, I'd gotten cramp. My left leg was now completely and utterly useless, I could no longer swim, I couldn't even tread water, I was just able to shout out rather pathetically, "Help! Cramp!" before disappearing under the water yet again. Had I swam out there alone I have no doubt that that would have been where I died, but at the last second Jadie reached me and pulled me back above the surface, keeping me there for several minutes until I regained feeling in my leg and was able to swim again. As grateful as I am for having her there to stop me from drowning, I couldn't help but tell her that the next time she tells someone there's a safety net to make damn sure it actually is a net and not just a rope.

If you told most people you enjoyed swimming, but were worried about getting eaten, then they would probably tell you to go to a swimming pool. When I was a kid that was fair enough, I enjoyed swimming in the pool, my dad used to take us to the Kingfisher Leisure Centre in Sudbury because it was much nicer than Crown Pools, our local pool. These days I'm not a fan of pools either because I see them as unhygienic, yes I know they fill them with chlorine but just because there's chemicals floating around in there it doesn't mean there's not piss as well, and it is also no guarantee that I won't swim into a disgusting mattered ball of hair left by some aquatic yeti of man who might have swam before me. Last time I went to Crown Pools with my girlfriend, we were in the water and I remember watching an elderly man as he swam laps around the pool, I watched as he hoovered the water into his mouth with one breath and then gozzed it back into the pool with the next, I wondered how much of the water I was swimming in had been in that man's mouth, and then I left the pool. Nope as far as I'm concerned, it's like sharing a big bath with a bunch of strangers and I'm not down for that, not unless I'm picking the strangers and I'm the only guy anyway.

When I was at primary school learning to swim was mandatory, as it should be. Children need to learn to swim in case one day their life depends on it. At Brookside Primary School we had a little pool and, on the way into it, everybody had to walk through some dark brown disinfectant, presumably to kill any random germs we might have been carrying on our feet. After our swimming lesson, on one occasion, everyone made their way back to the classroom, we were getting ourselves dried and dressed in there ready to continue with the school day. There was no segregation at that time, and at our age, between male and female students, we all did this together, supervised by the teachers. Thinking about it now I'm not convinced that should have been allowed and I'm sure it wouldn't be these days, a bunch of adults watching other people's children walk around in the buff, there's a register for people who do that. Anyway, as a child you don't consider these things, I was busy getting myself nice and dry, that was my only concern. I hurriedly walked over to where my clothes were waiting and shivered, it didn't take long to get cold once I was out of the pool and the air got to my skin. Taking out my towel ready to dry myself, I quickly whipped off my trunks and set to work drying my hair.

"No, no, no, no," I heard one of the teachers say in a very annoyed tone of voice, "what are you all doing?" I wasn't really paying attention; I was giving my hair a very thorough drying. "No, no, no, that's not how you do it, haven't your parents taught you anything?"

I spoke about the meanness of the teachers at my primary school before and, although this wasn't the teacher that made me rip out my tooth, it was another female teacher who had a reputation for being very cruel to her students.

The teacher continued her instruction on how to most efficiently to dry the naked human body as she observed our efforts, "You need to dry yourselves from the top down. If you start drying your bottom half first then all the water from the top will drip down making you wet again." she slowly walked around the room, going from child to child, "Wrong. Wrong. Wrong." her annoyance was more that apparent until finally she saw someone doing things in a way that met with her approval. "The only one of you doing the right thing…" she announced, "...is Chris." My ears pricked up as I heard my name and I froze looking out nervously from underneath the towel as I dried my hair. "Chris is the only one drying himself from the top down. Everyone turn and look at Chris and follow his example."

In any other aspect of the school day this may have been considered high praise indeed and perhaps I'd have even felt a little bit pleased with myself on hearing those words because, as far as I can recall, I was never pointed out as an example to follow in my life again. Even so, it's hard to be pleased with yourself when twenty or thirty people unexpectedly turn around to observe your naked form with uninvited eyes. I didn't move, I made no attempt to cover myself whatsoever, I felt paralyzed and became, in effect, a human statue, only my eyes moved like a haunted painting in a film, as I looked from face to face waiting for them to turn away so I could carry on. As soon as the class when back to drying themselves I threw my towel to the floor, the only part of myself I'd managed to dry was my hair but I didn't care anymore, I needed clothes and I was getting dressed whether I was soaking wet or not.

Luckily, I'm not the only one who gets into trouble with water, and on our trip to Malaga in 2019, my girlfriend Laura joined me in aquatic woe. It was the last full day of our holiday and we'd both wanted to enjoy a swim in the sea one last time before we left. It had been a really good week and the Spanish sun had been good to us so we were optimistic about our chances for warm weather that day despite the lower temperatures the weather forecast was predicting. We left our hotel and stepped onto the warm sand, the beach was crowded and we picked our way through the people until we approached the water, which was when we noticed that, although the beach was busy, nobody was in the sea. Laura and I watched the waves as they rose and crashed against the store, it certainly wasn't the tranquil waters we were used to but it our last opportunity to enjoy a swim in the sea and we decided that we might as well at least try going in.

I took my first step into the water, instantly the sheer coldness of it took my breath away but I moved forward determined not to be defeated. When the first wave hit me, I was surprised at the force of the impact which nearly took me off my feet and I began to realise just how hard it would be to make it out further with them pushing us back every few seconds. I quickly got into the habit of jumping with the waves as they approached to stay above them, and doing that repeatedly I was able to move out far enough to tread water.

I looked back to see where Laura was and found she was still struggling in the shallower waters, so I shouted back some words of encouragement for her to come and join me further out. Although Laura was unconvinced, she was able to, she still tried to reach me, and before long she was struck by a huge wave that not only stopped her in her tracks but sent her underwater too. A few seconds passed and I scanned the water unable to spot her, it doesn't take long for someone to vanish in water for it to feel like too long and I was anxious to see where she was. It seemed Laura had vanished without a trace until, finally, I caught sight of her again... well I was pretty sure it was her. Close to the shore, I could see a pair of feet wiggling above the surface, I was going to need more for a positive ID but given we were the only ones in the water there wasn't much doubt. The wave that hit her had knocked her under head first and pinned her there, I tried to wade through the water to reach her but as I did so suddenly she resurfaced gasping for air, I was relieved to see her face but my relief was short lived when, no sooner had she taken a breath, a second wave hit her in the face and sent her another twenty feet or so down the beach. With that second wave my initial concern had given way to laughter as I thought the comedic timing of that second wave was impeccable. Laura saw me laugh but she'd been more scared than I realised and did not see the funny side at all and, when I saw how upset she was, I headed back to shore to comfort her.

 I waded as fast as I could to reach Laura and dry land, by the time the water was around my waist, it occurred to me that, in my haste to see if my girlfriend was alright, I'd completely forgotten to keep an eye on any approaching waves, it also occurred to me that I hadn't dodged any at all since Laura had been hit the second time. I stopped dead in my tracks and turned around just to make sure I wasn't going to be caught off guard but it was too late, there in front of me, only inches from my face, was what I can only describe as a wall of water. "Oh shi…" that was as much of a sentence as I could manage before the wave hit me, it felt like running into a brick wall and I was knocked under the water before washing up on shore a few feet from Laura.

I coughed, the salt water burned my eyes as I climbed to my feet and rejoined my girlfriend. I must admit that turning around to face that wave felt more than a little bit like karma after laughing when it had happened to Laura, I guess the universe doesn't always give you a chance to say 'sorry'.

We gave up on swimming after that and had a quiet walk down the beach instead, which was probably what we should have done in the first place.

Christopher Moore

Tattoo

One of my favourite bands in the world has always been The Wildhearts. I was still at school when I first heard the band and, after twenty-five plus years, I'm still as much of a fan now as I was back then. They were one of the first bands I ever saw live, and since then I have seen them play all over the country more times than I can count. Their singer, Ginger Wildheart, is probably the most underrated songwriter of his generation and has written literally hundreds of songs that have almost become like a soundtrack to my life.

In 2013, Jadie and I went to see The Wildhearts play at London's Kentish Town Forum. Jadie had become a fan of their music as well after hearing me play their songs so many times over the years, we even had a fifteenth anniversary poster of the band's debut album, *Earth Versus the Wildhearts*, on our bedroom wall. We took an early train to London in order to make the most of the visit and by lunch time we'd already checked into our hotel for the night and located the venue, so we set off to explore the local area before the gig. It was fun walking around Kentish Town with Jadie, taking in the various shops and bars as we excitedly awaited the evening's entertainment.

Around midafternoon, we happened upon a little tattoo shop not far from the venue called Scratchline Tattoo and, as I looked in the window, I decided that since we had some time to kill, maybe I could get some new ink. The idea of having me get a new tattoo wasn't what my wife had in mind for our afternoon in London and she was apprehensive to say the least. Every time I had gotten a new tattoo during our time together, I'd had to convince Jadie to go along with the idea, I wasn't covered with ink, far from it, but still she was adamant that I had enough and didn't need anymore, so I reassured her, as I always did, that this would absolutely and unequivocally be the last time I would ever venture into a tattoo studio. It never was. I'm quite an impulsive person so, even though I would make a promise with the best of intentions, keeping it once I got a new idea in my head, was easier said than done.

We entered the tattoo shop after I'd sunk a few beers, this is never the best of ideas but I wasn't blind drunk, just a little bit tipsy, and I had what I thought was a really good design. I decided, because we were in London to see The Wildhearts, that perhaps some artwork connected with the band would be good, Ginger had a solo record called *Valor Del Corazon* some years previously, which I'd always thought had a nice ring to it as a title, so I went with that. Because I'd had a couple of drinks I concluded, for safety's sake, I would be better off going for the English translation of that album title which was 'Strength of Heart'. On entering the tattoo shop we found it empty apart from two members of staff, the attractive rock chick working on reception and the tattoo artist, who was also female. I spoke to the receptionist first and I remember being struck by her eyebrows, which she'd removed and drawn back on.

For the entirety of my adult life this whole female eyebrow thing has been something I've never properly understood the concept of. Yes, I do understand that maybe your eyebrows may not look exactly as you might like, maybe they're a bit wild or maybe they need grooming in some way, I can imagine that being as issue which you might benefit from correcting. However, when you look in a mirror and decide you can do better than your natural, real eyebrows with some sort of pen, then shave them off and start doodling on your face, well, can that ever be considered anything less than a breakdown? And if this is really an acceptable practice, why isn't it something that is used universally across the board? For example, if a man starts to go bald why doesn't he just reach for the nearest marker pen and start colouring? If I were to shave my beard off and decide I'd made a huge mistake, could I just draw it back on? Or if I was on a date and the lady mentioned she liked a man with chest hair, could I just pop to the toilet with a biro and sort it out? How are those things any different? It's a confusing world sometimes.

Anyway, I spoke to Eyebrows on reception and told her of the design I had in mind, for a small tattoo it was fairly expensive but we were in London and everything is more expensive when you're in a capital city. I didn't mind paying the extra as long as the end result was worth it, so I told Eyebrows that I'd like to go ahead. The tattoo artist was a foreign lady, I can't remember where it was, she came from but I recall she had a nice accent, and my wife and I took a seat in reception whilst she prepared the stencil. After ten to fifteen minutes it was ready and, after Jadie and I both checked it, she proceeded with the tattoo on my right forearm.

A short while later, with my shiny new tattoo completed and my arm wrapped in clingfilm, we left Scratchline and headed over to a pub close to the venue, called the Assembly House, for a cold beverage and possibly something to eat as well. We chose a table in close proximity to the bar, sat down with our beers and began to peruse the menu. Only a matter of minutes after we sat down, the door opened, and two members of The Wildhearts walked in, it seemed my day was getting better and better. From our table we watched as guitarist CJ and bassist Jon Poole stood at the end of the bar waiting to be served, I never liked interrupting someone in the street just because I knew who they were, but in a pub setting after a few beers I figured it was probably alright to just say hello, so I left Jadie at the table and walked over.

I'd met Ginger Wildheart several times in the past but this was the first time I'd spoken to anyone else in the band, and I was pleased to discover that they were very friendly guys and more than happy to talk to me for a few minutes, or at least they were polite enough to give that impression.

Noticing the clingfilm on my arm after a few minutes of conversation, CJ gestured towards it and asked, "You're a bit overprotective of your tattoos aren't you mate?"

I looked back down at my arm having momentarily forgotten all about the tattoo before responding, "Yeah I'm like a sixties housewife with a new sofa, I like to keep the plastic on." CJ, who had just taken a sip of his beer, almost choked with laughter.

Things were going well so before I wore out my welcome, I quickly called Jadie over and got her to snap a quick picture of me with The Wildhearts, then we left them to their drinks and returned to our table chuffed that we'd run into them.

A few hours, and a few pints, deeper into the evening and we were still having a great time, Jadie's annoyance at my unplanned trip to the tattoo studio was forgotten for the time being at least and we were only a few hours away from an amazing live set by The Wildhearts, spirits were high. A song by Nine Inch Nails was playing in the background as we drank, hearing any NIN song always made me think of another song of theirs, a track called 'Every Day Is Exactly the Same'. EDIETS (great abbreviation) is a fantastic song, but it always made me laugh despite that fact that the song itself in dark and brooding. The thing is, in the opening lyrics Trent Reznor mispronounces a word and once you notice that then you can't unhear it. The line in the song as written, goes as follows, "I think I used to have a purpose, but then again that might have been a dream." however, it sounds like Trent's singing, "I think I used to have a porpoise." and, because the lyric is so early on in the song, it could be perceived that the whole song is an incredibly sad tale about a rock singer who has misplaced his dolphin. I shared my theory on Reznor's fondness for aquatic life with Jadie before all the talk about the ocean made me realise it was time for me to visit the little boys' room.

Still chuckling to myself I got to my feet and headed to the bathroom. Personally, I'm not the kind of guy who likes to use public bathrooms, I like privacy and, no matter where you go, the gents' toilets, especially in pubs, are not designed to give you any privacy whatsoever. If I was redesigning the men's bathroom today, I'd do three things, firstly, I'd make a proper divide between urinals, so if someone did take the stall next to me it wouldn't be an issue. Secondly, I'd pipe in the sound of running water throughout, maybe a thunderstorm soundtrack or something, which would remove the awkward silence of the urinal, help you pee if you were struggling and, in the event that you had a performance issue, nobody would realise you actually hadn't been. And finally, I'd get rid of any and all 'toilet guys', those arseholes who stand by the sinks with some cheap fragrances expecting a tip when you go to wash your hands, I mean what the absolute fuck are those guys for? There's nothing worse than standing at the urinal and trying to pee with some toilet guy's eyes burning into the back of my skull, as if it's my fault they work in a toilet. The amount of times I've left a public bathroom and tipped one of those men a pound for actively stopping me from being able to piss is unbelievable. Is it really too much to ask to be able to go to the toilet in peace? I'm sure that guy I water bombed in the Christchurch Park toilets would agree further measures could be taken.

After we'd finished urinating, I spoke to Jon again, you have to wait until after, never strike up a conversation with a man during, even if you have already met, whatever it is you need to discuss can wait. As we chatted and washed our hands, I decided to peel the clingfilm off of my new tattoo and take a look at the masterpiece I had acquired. I stared at the tattoo in the mirror and, with the writing in the reflection being backwards and my being a little drunk, all I could tell was something didn't seem quite right, but what exactly it was, well that eluded me.

"Looks good." said Jon, glancing over as he shook the water from his hands into the sink.

I wasn't so sure, "Yeah, but…" I trailed off unsure what the ending to my sentence was. The mirror wasn't doing me any favours in seeing the problem, so I looked down and read the text directly off of my skin, 'Strength of Heart' I said slowly, 'Strength of Heart'. Ever so gradually it dawned on me, the reason it didn't look right was that I was missing a letter, the mother flipping 'T' in the word 'Strength' was not present in place between the 'G' and 'H', how could I not have noticed the mistake before the tattoo was completed? I'd checked it, we'd all checked it. I thought back to earlier in the day in the tattoo studio, I had only quickly scanned the design without really paying that much attention, Jadie was dyslexic and so, though no fault of her own, probably wouldn't have spotted the mistake anyway and the tattooist wasn't English so was writing in her second language, I should have paid more attention. "No, no, no, no, no." I said to myself, my voice getting progressively louder as the seriousness of my error stared back at me from my now permanently marked skin.

Jon turned back from the hand dryer, "What's wrong?" he asked.

"She's only missed out the fucking 'T'." I was in total shock as I stood in front of the mirror wearing an expression not unlike that of a goldfish. Jon, who had a misspelled tattoo himself, said he thought it was funnier to just leave it as it was so I could tell the story to my friends for a cheap laugh, I did not agree, I could think of easier ways to deliver a punchline than that. Knowing I'd feel that little twinge of regret every time I looked at my arm for that day forward, there was only one thing for it, I had to get back to the tattoo shop. I ran out of the toilet as fast as I could, I clambered up the stairs using both my hands and feet to scramble up like some sort of wild animal and then, upon reaching the top I sprinted through the pub, pausing only briefly to let Jadie know I was missing my flipping 'T', before leaving her in the bar and taking off at breakneck speed down the street.

Out of breath I burst through the door of Scratchline Tattoo, I was like a man possessed, I stormed up to the reception desk where the tattooist waited and, before she could say anything, I thrust my arm under her nose, "You've misspelt my tattoo!"

The tattooist looked at her work and realised what she'd done, I could see from her expression she was mortified, "Oh my god, I'm so sorry. English isn't my first language, I'm so sorry, we'll fix it, of course." That, at least, was something. Although I was very angry, in all honesty I was angrier at myself than I was at anyone else, I couldn't believe I'd gotten the English translation of the album title just to avoid not noticing a spelling error in a foreign language while under the influence, and then I'd gone and missed the mistake written in English. The title sounded so much better in Spanish as well and in the cold light of day, when I sobered up, I didn't even like the English translation. Later I discovered Ginger had misspelled the title anyway and it should have read 'Valor DE Corazon' not 'Del' as appeared on the artwork, so either way I'd have ended up looking illiterate to someone.

I sat down with artist who was unsure how to go about adding the 'T' without ruining the spacing between the letters, the spacing was the least of my concerns, after much deliberation, in the end all she could do was go for it and to be honest, it wasn't could have been much worse, unless it was pointed out to them, most people never even noticed there was anything wrong. Even so, I immediately disliked the tattoo because, when I looked at my arm, all I saw was the mistake, the free t-shirt and hugs I received by way of an apology from both the tattooist and her friend Eyebrows, did little to make me feel better.

After leaving Scratchline for the second time I returned to the Assembly House to find my wife who, understandably, wasn't pleased to have been abandoned in a random London pub. At least Jadie didn't have a typo on her arm though, so in my opinion she was doing better than me and she was also able to deliver a scathing 'I told you so'. A short time later I ran into Jon again who invited me to his table where I got a drink and regaled the crowd with the story of my tattoo disaster, much to their amusement. In fact, I stayed there so long Jadie had to come and find me, which again didn't do anything for her mood. Luckily The

Wildhearts were so good we soon forgot about the days mishaps and everything seemed right with the world again, that was, unless I looked at my arm.

Six years after that day I finally got that tattoo covered with my own design and am, once again, able to look at my arm without feeling like a complete idiot.

Transferable Skills

At the start of this book I talked briefly about when my father used to cut my hair as a child, I never thought I'd do the same thing with my own daughter but there's moments in life when even the worst of ideas feel like inspired moments of pure genius.

It was one of those rare occasions when I'd actually made it home from work on time, we'd had dinner and my wife, Jadie, was getting ready to take a nap before her evening shift at Tesco. This was pretty much a daily routine for us, she would go and get an hour in bed and I would wake her up with a fresh cup of coffee when it was time for her to get ready to go. On this occasion, as Jadie made her way to the bedroom, I'd made a passing comment about how long Faith's hair was getting, it had been a fair while since she'd been to the hairdressers and her hair now reached halfway down her back. In agreement, Jadie told me she would take Faith to the hairdressers as soon as she had a chance, before going into the bedroom and closing the door behind her.

Back in the living room, I sat down on the sofa with my eldest daughter Christina and watched television. Faith was sitting on the floor in front of me and, looking over at her, I couldn't help but think to myself how much better her hair would look if it was cut to shoulder length. I glanced back at the television trying to put the thought out of my mind, Jadie had said she'd take care of it and that was the end of that... or at least it should have been. I looked over to Faith once again anxious to be a good husband and father and solve the problem without the need for my wife to have to stress about anything, I didn't want to give her another job to do, there must be a way for me to resolve this myself sooner rather than later. Now I'm not technically a qualified hairdresser, having never taken a course or acquired the correct piece of paper, but one thing I certainly did have was the enthusiasm to help... and a sturdy pair of scissors. I mean how hard could it be? I had life experience, at work if anyone required anything cutting out, anything at all, I was the man, so what if I was used to a scalpel rather than a pair of scissors, cutting is cutting, you can't tell me that it isn't a transferable skill. I smiled as I looked at my daughter and I pictured Jadie's happy and grateful face as she left for work knowing that I'd saved her time and money by eliminating the hairdresser from the equation. I was going to save the day.

Minutes later after vocalizing my thoughts to my daughters, and noting their objections, I had Faith sat comfortably in a dining room chair in front of me and a pair of scissors in my hand.

"Dad I really don't think this is a good idea." Christina said with a concerned expression on her face, "Maybe you should talk to mum about it."

I shot my eldest daughter a look, a look that told her without the use of words that everything was under control, and then just to be certain, I reassured her verbally as well,

"Christina, it's fine. You worry too much, trust me. I've got this under control."

Christina was unconvinced and tried once again to reason with her deluded parent, "But you really shouldn't be…"

I cut her off mid-sentence, "It's alright, by the time your mum is out of bed it'll be done and she'll have a lovely surprise. Look at Faith, she's not worried, she trusts me."

Undeterred by my best efforts to put her mind at ease, Christina couldn't help trying to change my mind once more, "But she's not old enough to know better Dad."

I smiled at Christina, impressed by her efforts to do what she considered to be the right thing, at her age I'd have pulled up a chair and hoped for disaster but not her, she was always a responsible and well behaved child, who knows where she got that from. Still, before I commenced the cut, I gave her a final few words of comfort, "Just sit there and watch how hairdressing is done, you might learn a thing or two." and with that I turned my attention back to her sister.

Faith sat perfectly still on the chair as I carefully brushed her hair to make sure it was tangle free and as even as possible to cut, "Alright Faith, I'm all done brushing, I think we're ready to cut your hair." I was extremely confident I could apply the skills I'd learnt at work to the simple task of cutting hair however I could see from the look on Christina's face, as I gathered a fair clump of Faith's hair together and moved the scissors towards it, she did not share this confidence. And, after I'd made my first cut, suddenly neither did I.

Sometimes you have to do something before you realise that it's not as easy as it might first appear, it only took me one cut to realise this but, regrettably, that one cut had taken off a noticeable chunk of my daughter's hair, I had no choice but to continue. For my daughter, who sat as good as gold on that chair, full of trust and admiration for her father's ability to style her hair, for her, I probably should have left the words that escaped my mouth next as a harmless thought in my head.

"Uh oh," I said as I watched the freshly cut hair fall towards the ground, "I'm in over my head here!"

The thing was, I hadn't expected the hair to move so much with the blades of the scissors as I cut, the hair got pushed out of place making it hard to achieve an even cut, my confidence vanished in a split second. Of course, my lost confidence transferred very quickly to my youngest daughter, who was no longer sure that her father had the ability to back up the claims he'd made so cockily earlier, so much so that she changed her mind about the whole thing.

"I don't want my hair cut anymore," Faith said getting out of her seat, "I'm going to go and play."

"It's ok baby, don't worry," I replied, doing my best to backtrack from my previous statement, "I was only joking, I need to finish it." Reluctantly Faith sat back down and, after taking a deep breath, I continued in the hope that the more I cut the easier it would get. As the minutes passed my confidence, once again, began to grow. I trimmed a little here, I made a slight adjustment there, I checked it from different angles, it really was starting to look pretty good even if I do say so myself and I began to think that my initial assessment of the task had been pretty accurate, qualifications are overrated.

Fifteen to twenty minutes later I stood back and looked proudly at Faith with her brand-new shoulder length haircut, "There, all done," I said, brushing the hair from her shoulders, "it looks fantastic."

Excitedly Faith popped up from her seat like a little rocket and ran to have a look in the bathroom mirror. Christina stared at me coldly, "Dad, it does not look fantastic!"

"Shh, it IS fantastic!" I insisted.

"Dad," Faith called from the bathroom, "Dad, I can't see properly." I walked into the bathroom and held her up to the mirror.

"There you go. What do you think? Do you like it?"

"Yes, thank you Daddy." I put her down and she ran off to her bedroom to play. That was the review that mattered to me, as long as Faith was happy, I could consider myself a success. I returned to the living room, picked up the freshly cut hair from the floor and hoovered the remaining bits up just as my alarm went off, it was time for Jadie to get ready for work so I went to the kitchen and made her coffee.

I swung the bedroom door open, "Wake up, it's almost time for work. Here's your coffee." I placed the cup on the bedside table as Jadie stirred from her nap. "How are you doing?" Groggily she let me know she was alright, and I continued on cheerfully. "Guess what I did while you were asleep…" Jadie's expression quickly changed to one of concern as she looked up at me, she knew me too well.

"Oh god Chris, what have you done now?" I wasn't sure I appreciated her tone. What I'd done might have been really nice and helpful, for all she knew I could have won the lottery and was waking her up with the news we were millionaires, I wasn't of course but I don't think it's fair to assume the worst. I chose to ignore the negative tone in her voice and I proceeded, making sure I still sounded upbeat.

"I've sorted Faith's hair out, so now you don't have to take her to get it cut." I was careful to phrase this statement in such a way that it appeared I had done exactly what she wanted me to do knowing full well that, had I talked to her about it beforehand, she would have told me unequivocally not to even think about going near our daughter's head with a pair of scissors.

My wife did not look grateful for my help, in fact, as she looked at me, I became increasingly convinced the scary look in her eyes could possibly be interpreted as anger. "Please tell me you're joking." she said quietly, a little too quietly for my liking. Was there the slightest possibility I had misjudged the entire situation? I was starting to wonder… Remain upbeat, that's what I told myself, if I'm enthusiastic about things maybe she'll pick up on that energy. With that ethos in mind I called Faith into the bedroom to show her waiting mother her amazing new hairstyle. I smiled as large a smile as I could muster as Faith entered the room which probably made me look slightly demented, needs must. Jadie sat up in bed and Faith gave her little twirl before joining her on the bed, "Jesus, how much did you cut off?" she asked, it was a fair question, when I said I'd cut Faith's hair all Jadie probably expected was a little trim, but it was now probably about a foot shorter than it was before she had her nap, the difference was dramatic. I watched as my wife examined Faith's hair in disbelief and I'll say this for her, she was thorough, "Chris it's awful, it's all uneven. Why did you think you could cut her hair?" she stared at me in disappointment, it was the look of a wife who'd endured her impulsive husband for too long and, as I spotted the tears in her eyes, I began to feel truly awful.

Even though inside I really did feel bad for upsetting Jadie, I genuinely believed I had done a good job, in fact, I still do. The problem was, and is, that I seem to be the only one who holds that opinion. Unwilling to go down without a fight I persevered, "No it's fine. She looks lovely."

"It's not lovely is it. It's all over the place. It slopes up on one side for god's sake." a tear rolled down Jadie's cheek and I was reminded how my own mother had cried all those years earlier when my father cut my hair. My wife's critique of my handiwork had not gone unnoticed by Faith who, by this point, had changed her mind about her new haircut and was now as upset with her father as everyone else. Nobody enjoys seeing the people they love upset, and when Faith became worried about her hair, I felt worse than I can begin to explain. Jadie reassured Faith that she would take her to the hairdressers to get it fixed as soon as possible as I returned to the living room in disgrace. Maybe the execution had been slightly flawed, maybe it was uneven in places, but as first attempts went, I was sure it could have been a lot worse. I offered all three of them haircuts from time to time over the following years but for some reason nobody ever took me up on them again.

Lost in London

      In March of 2016 I was headed to London for another gig, this time it was with my best friend Jason and his friend Clive, it was my first-time meeting Clive but since this trip he has become one of my closest friends. We were all on our way to see a band called Heck, formally known as Baby Godzilla, who were well known for their frantic live shows. I'd seen them play a few times previously, first hearing them as a support band for The Wildhearts and then later venturing out to see them in other places. I loved their live shows because of the energy they had, you never knew what was going to happen at a Heck show because they didn't confine themselves to the stage, they came over the barrier and into the crowd, they climbed on anything and everything and they had a complete disregard for health and safety. They were both a roadie and a venues worst nightmare and I thought they were amazing. At one show Matt, who was the singer /guitarist, used me as his microphone stand, I stood there holding the mic up for him as he screamed in my face. At another, Johnny, the other singer /guitarist, walked up to me on the front row, handed me his guitar and then left. As I held the guitar in my hands, I couldn't believe my luck, to actually be given a guitar by the band was just unbelievable and the crowd around me we're dumbfounded. When Johnny left the stage a bouncer came over and, assuring me I would get the guitar back at the end of the show, he offered to take it off me and store it by the side of the stage, I refused as I felt better keeping hold of it myself. Around ten minutes later, to my surprise, Johnny came back onto the stage and asked me for his guitar. I was shocked and hesitated in my response, the crowd around me reacted faster though and rallied around me, they told Johnny that they all witnessed him giving me the guitar and he wasn't getting it back. Unexpectedly confronted with an angry audience, Johnny found himself having to justify his actions and plead for his guitar.

"I'm really sorry guys but I need that guitar, I'm a poor musician, it's all I've got." The hecklers weren't backing down no matter how much Johnny apologised, he looked at me with desperation in his eyes and he pleaded one more time. I felt bad for him, there had clearly been a misunderstanding and so I was left with a choice, keep the guitar and leave with the ultimate souvenir or return it to its rightful owner.

I gave the guitar one last look and I tossed it back up to the stage where Johnny caught it, "Don't worry about it mate, I've got plenty of guitars at home." I shouted. Johnny tore the strings off the guitar and handed them to me, thanking me for returning it. It would have been a nightmare to try and hang onto it for the whole gig anyway, which is not to say I wasn't more than a little gutted because I was, but I'm not going to take a man's guitar.

At another show I attended, I was quite drunk and I accidently spilled a lot of beer over the band's merchandise stand, I bought a snapback cap to say sorry and they were really nice about the whole incident. It was always good to see them and it was definitely a shame when the band split up.

So that's who we were going to see, we sat on the train heading towards London, drinking beer and having a laugh. When we arrived at our destination we checked into our hotel, in the room there were only two beds for the three of us so Jason and Clive agreed to share one and I would have my own. I had slept in a bed with Jason before the Download festival a few years previously so I figured it was someone else's turn. We left the hotel as quickly as possible after dropping our bags off and carried on drinking until it was time for the gig. During that time, we mentioned that it might be a good idea to go to Camden the next day before we went home and have a wander around, depending on how we felt when we woke up of course.

The chances of feeling capable of doing anything the following morning were looking increasingly slim, before we even walked into the venue, I was drunk, we all were, but looking back on that night now, I'd definitely say I wasn't handling my drink as well as my friends. As soon as the doors were open, we hit the bar, and I began the process of drunkenly flirting with every woman unlucky enough to catch my eye. I was obviously a complete mess, but at the time, and with that many beers inside me, I believed myself to be the most handsome and charming man in the place. While Jason and Clive watched the first few bands, I spent that time talking to a beautiful girl at the bar. I was still married at this time and would never have really considered cheating on my wife but I'd been with her so long it was nice to be able to think, for a short time at least, that somebody else still found me attractive, even if in reality the woman in question was more than likely looking for the first opportunity to walk away. Anyway, I was busy telling this girl what a great guy I was when Jason came up to the bar to order a beer on his way to the toilet, "Jaaaaay," I slurred, "will you tell this lady what a good guy I am?"

"He is," started Jason without thinking, "I should know, I was his best man." With that he turned and started to walk away.

The girl laughed as my jaw hit the floor, "Unbelievable." I sighed holding up my hands in exasperation.

Moments later Heck took the stage and I quickly made my excuses to the girl I was talking to, who was probably quite relieved, and I fought my way through the crowd to rejoin my friends at the front. The band were on great form and we were going crazy in the mosh pit along with the rest of the crowd. With my inhibitions ever so slightly lowered by the alcohol in my system, I decided it would be a fantastic idea if I were to start crowd surfing and, after making sure my friends were watching, I clambered up onto the stage with the band before launching myself off backwards into the crowd. The next day Jason showed me a video he'd taken of my crowd surf where I was held aloft by a sea of people one minute, and then suddenly dropped the next, it looks like I just fold in half at the waist and then I disappeared completely into the crowd, absorbed by the horde. It was a good first attempt but it was by no means perfect, so I tried again. And again. And again. Too many times, each one less successful than the last with the crowds dwindling enthusiasm for my efforts making them less willing to hold me up.

By the time the band left the stage, we were all sweat soaked and exhausted, but ultimately on a high from what had been an outstanding show and, as the house lights came on, we joyfully exited the venue into the freezing cold night air. Now when I say freezing, trust me when I say it absolutely was freezing, immediately my nipples turned into two rock hard little bullets grazing against the inside of my dripping wet Baby Godzilla t-shirt. I folded my arms and shivered, with no coat to speak of, a sweaty t-shirt and a nasty frost in the air, I was vulnerable to the elements and needed to get somewhere warm fast, preferably another bar but, given the circumstances, anywhere would be better than outside.

The first place we spotted that was open was not strictly a bar… it was a sex shop. It must have taken us all of half a second to decide it was close enough before we hurried inside, keen to warm our cold bodies against a radiator or perhaps a toasty inflatable, were one to be readily available, although the act of inflating a new companion would likely be warming in of itself. Once inside we found we weren't the only customers seeking shelter from the unforgiving night air, across the store a small group of girls perused the shelves on their way to wherever it was they were headed. Needing a destination ourselves, and with no better plan springing to mind, Jason went over and asked them where they were heading, that was how we ended up at a gay bar.

So there we were, Jason, Clive and myself, sat in a quiet corner of the gay bar, the girls we had arrived with had, for some reason, not wanted to stay with the three random men they met skulking around a sex shop in the middle of the night, and they'd gone and sat somewhere else. I've never been particularly comfortable around homosexual men, just because it's not something I identify with, I know that's not a particularly politically correct thing to say these days but I'm a socially awkward person and there's not too many places I do feel like I belong. Being in the gay bar made me uncomfortable, in the same way I wouldn't feel comfortable visiting a stranger's house, or a ballroom dance class, or a gym, and it was for that reason that I didn't really enjoy being in a bar intended for a different clientele than myself. Clive was of a similar opinion and sat moodily with his hood up as we drank, it wasn't until the DJ played a Craig David song that he mellowed out again. As we got used to our surroundings we got back to having fun, Jason had started taking selfies on his phone of the three of us but strangely this hadn't gone down well with a group of queens nearby who, rather aggressively, accused my friend of taking pictures of them. Why they thought he was doing so, and what purpose they imagined he might have for the pictures, was a mystery, even now the whole thing makes no sense to me. Eventually the argument was diffused without any punches, or slaps, being thrown and we moved to another part of the club away from the troublemakers.

Shortly after, the DJ started playing some decent tunes and we were inspired to dance, I had climbed onto the podium to show off my dance moves while Jason and Clive stuck to the dancefloor below me. If I was out of my comfort zone before, just being in the club, I really had no place dancing on an elevated platform centre stage, damn that DJ and his funky beats. It was while I was up there making shapes that, inadvertently, some beer spilled out of my glass and landed on Jason who did not appreciate the 'golden shower' I had given him; yes I know that's not the correct term for a beer spill from above, but I feel that it works here just as well as it does in the traditional sense, and it's my book so... Jason took my 'golden shower' and, although he was a little annoyed, he asked me to be more careful and carried on busting a move. Now when you've had a drink, it can often be the case that you will react in an inappropriate fashion, or at least in a manner not in keeping with your usual responses, to any given situation. That was the case here. I should have apologised to my friend and got back to looking like a tit on the podium, but instead I spilled beer on Jason again, this time intentionally. The second time I performed this act it wasn't so easily brushed off as the first, especially not with me laughing like an idiot at my increasingly moist associate, but the angrier he got, the funnier my alcohol-soaked mind found it. When I spilt beer on him a third time, a now soaking wet Jason unsurprisingly snapped and told me, in no uncertain terms, to "Fuck off!" and retreated to the bathroom, with Clive in tow, to dry off.

As I stood there alone, on a podium in the middle of a gay bar, with my beverage severely depleted, and my best friend angry at me, I realised that I hadn't been being funny at all, I'd been being a bit of a dickhead. It was a sobering thought. With my head lowered in shame I stepped carefully down from the podium and downed the remnants of my beer; it was time for me to leave. As I walked through the exit and back out into the street, I had momentarily forgotten that I was somewhere in the middle of London and, not only did I have no way of getting back to my actual home in Suffolk, I didn't have any idea where the hotel was that we were staying in, or even what it was called.

On leaving the bar I turned left and started walking. Where I was actually going to hadn't even entered my mind, I was upset by Jason's outburst and was feeling very bad about myself, I just wanted to get as far away from everyone as possible. It was the early hours of the morning and the temperature had dropped even lower than it had been when we were in the club, I could see the parked cars lining the street were all frozen solid and I, once again, cursed myself for only coming out in a t-shirt. In order to generate a bit of warmth I pulled my arms inside the t-shirt and cuddled my torso, it helped, but not to the extent I needed, even the vast amount of alcohol in my system wasn't enough to keep the cold at bay. I looked down the road and realised for the first time, that I was completely and totally lost, so much so that I couldn't even retrace my steps. Removing an arm from my torso, I felt in my pocket for my phone, I was now in an emergency survival situation and I knew, from watching vast amounts of hours of Bear Grylls programs, that my best shot of getting out of the cold alive was to call for help. Sadly, when I looked at my screen, I found the battery had died, briefly I remembered an episode of *Man vs. Wild* where Bear had used the battery from his phone to start a fire, I'd leave that as a last resort and decided instead to keep moving. I figured the best place to go was Liverpool Street Station, that was where my train home would depart from so, to me, it was the only place that made sense. I walked for hours hoping to find some sort of shelter or a familiar landmark to aid me in my navigation but I saw nothing that gave me a clear indication where the station actually was, in all honesty it could have been around the next corner or fifty miles away for all I knew. Eventually, out of sheer exhaustion, I decided to find somewhere to sleep. The best option available appeared to be an old phone box which, although dirty and littered with the telephone numbers of various escorts, at least provided some protection from the ice-cold wind, so I climbed inside and there and, slumped in a corner, I got a couple of hours much needed sleep.

Jason was dry, well as dry as he could be after being bathed in a frothy amber liquid by someone, he trusted not to moisten him up in such a fashion. He was due to share a bed with Clive later in the night and he hoped he could count on his other friend not to spray him with any further liquids while he slept. Jason and Clive returned to the dancefloor and found the third member of their group, me, had done a Houdini and was no longer anywhere to be found. At first they weren't overly concerned by this and began a search of the premises covering all the likely places a straight man was likely to be in a gay club, such as the bar, the bathroom (cubicle), the few seats that were available and the area outside the front door in case I'd needed some air. After this initial investigation turned up no leads, they decided to call me however, because my phone had died, they could only get through to voicemail. It was a tough situation for them both to be in, but after searching some more they did the only thing they could, and returned to the hotel in the hope that was where I'd gone. When they arrived back at the hotel they had found it empty, by now they were very worried about where I was and tried to call me multiple times, as well as checking the area outside the hotel on the off chance I was nearby, but it was all to no avail, in the end all they could do was go to sleep and hope that by morning I would reappear. So, Jason and Clive retired to bed and, even though my bed was empty, they still decided to stick to our prearranged sleeping agreement and slept in the same bed together in case I returned. Whether they were thinking of me, or were just inspired by the club we had been in, I really couldn't say.

As the rising sun poured through the glass in my cramped little telephone box, my eyes blinked open and I squinted through the morning light at my surroundings. "For fucks sake," I groaned, my head throbbing, "I'm still here!" although I did recall falling asleep in that location, a big part of me had hoped that when I woke up it would have been a dream. No such luck. As I staggered to my feet my whole body was aching and stiff from my night on the streets, not only that but it was still bloody freezing. I checked my pockets, as I always did after a night out, my wallet, keys and phone were all still present which provided me with a minimal amount of relief, I stared at the phone, "Come on, turn on." I pleaded under my breath as I held down the power button and, by some miracle, it worked. In the thirty seconds or so that I had before the battery died, I searched for directions to Liverpool Street Station and I was pleased to see I wasn't that far away all things considered. As my phone abruptly turned itself back off, I turned in the direction it had indicated and prepared myself to cover another few miles as fast as possible.

Meanwhile, back at the hotel, Jason and Clive stirred from their slumber, although I'm sure they did their best to stay separate in the night and the following is nothing more than conjecture, I'd say Clive was probably the big spoon, just like John Candy in *Planes, Trains and Automobiles*. The first thing my friends did upon waking was to check my bed to see if I'd appeared, needless to say it hadn't been touched, so once again they tried to call me and, once again, I did not answer. From their point of view, well from mine as well, this was not a good situation, they were a man down and, as far as they were aware, anything could have happened to me. Unable to make contact with me, my friends were out of options and, in desperation, they reached out to some other people to see if they had heard from me, one of the people that they spoke to was my wife, Jadie, who hit the roof and told Jason that he had to call the police straight away.

Back home in Kesgrave, a whole new machine had been set in motion. Jadie was absolutely frantic with worry, her husband, the father of her children, was missing. London could be a very dangerous place, especially at night and her mind had immediately turned to the worst-case scenario. In no time at all the word had spread to anyone and everyone connected to me in any way at all, except for me of course, I was still completely oblivious that I was becoming the subject of a man hunt, but everyone else was involved in the search. My parents were on the case and they were harassing the fuzz for results, my sisters were busy calling every hospital in London and even Heck, the band themselves, were posting about me on social media. Jadie was getting messages of support all over the place and me, well, I was freezing my tits off.

After walking for what seemed like forever by sheer luck, I had made it to Liverpool Street Station. This was where we needed to be to catch our train home that afternoon, so I was confident this would be the first place my friends would come in the morning to look for me, surely it wouldn't be long before they showed up. Liverpool Street Station is, unfortunately, open air, it has no roof, so it was just as cold inside the station as it was outside. Shivering I paced up and down to keep warm, I imagined my friends' arrival, I pictured them showing up with my bag containing my jumper and my coat and I fantasized about wrapping myself up warm in those thick layers. Nobody came. I wished there were some battery life left in my phone so I could at least call them and find out where they were.

At the hotel, the police had arrived. They separated Jason and Clive and interviewed them individually about my disappearance, as if they themselves were under suspicion.

This is where our recollection of events differed. Remember earlier I mentioned we'd talked about the possibility of going to Camden before we went home? Well

Jason and Clive would tell you that it was decided that we were definitely doing that, however, I will tell you categorically that we weren't and, even if we were, at this point any plans we had would have been well and truly changed. Even so the lads told the law we were planning on going to Camden, so the cops said if that was the plan I would probably head there and so they should do that as well. It did not occur to either my friends or the police that making to our train home might have been a priority for me in my circumstances, rather than having an aimless stroll around Camden on my own, so instead of coming to find me at the train station, Jason and Clive headed to Camden to search for me… and to have a little breakfast.

    Back at Liverpool Street I was having breakfast too, I needed to get out of the cold so I went in to the McDonald's on the corner for a sausage and egg muffin. Inside I found there were iPhone chargers at some of the tables, the one closest to me was broken, so I walked around the restaurant and tried them all, every single one of them had been destroyed and were, as such, useless. After that I went to buy a power pack so I could charge my phone from that, but they were too expensive and would need an initial charge before I could use them anyway, making them worthless. I gave up as I didn't want to stray too far from the station in case the others finally turned up, or I got lost again. With that in mind, I went back to pacing briskly from one end of the station to the other to keep warm.

    It was somewhere between one and two in the afternoon when the train was due and by that time I was seriously pissed off, I couldn't believe that my friends hadn't even thought to come to the train station and I had never been so cold in my life. I waited impatiently for my train's platform to be announced and as soon as it was, I headed straight for it, all I wanted was to be on that train and on my way home. I approached the barrier with my ticket in hand when I heard a familiar voice from the crowd, "Chris! Chris!" I turned around just in time to see my friends emerge from out of a crowd of people. My anger immediately dissipated when I saw the relief on their faces to have found me and I was happy beyond words to see them, as soon as they reached me Clive just reached in and hugged me, I'd only met him the day before, maybe the combination of a gay bar and a night in bed with Jason had changed him but I didn't mind, the relief, and the hug, was mutual. It was an emotional few minutes, even more so when I saw they were carrying my bags, as soon as we were on the train I was throwing on layers of clothing while they told me about the police and the extent of the search that had been going on for me. I don't think I really believed anyone had been looking for me at all, that was until I plugged my phone into the charger on the train and finally switched it on. I had never had so many notifications, there were messages from all over the place and I was, for the want of a better word, flabbergasted. I had a lot of calls to make.

When we made it back to Ipswich Station, Jadie was there to pick me up. The first thing she did, when I was in range, was punch me in the arm, before giving me the biggest hug I think she'd ever given me in her life, I wasn't sure she ever wanted to let go and, as wonderful as it felt to receive, I was only a few short hours removed from Clive's embrace and that was a tough hug to beat. My wife went on to tell me, in great detail, how scared she'd been that I'd been hurt and how worried everyone had been about me. I felt awful for what she'd been through and I also felt extremely lucky to have so many people in my life that cared about me that much.

Christopher Moore

The World's Hottest Vodka

I've spent a lot of time drinking in various pubs, bars and clubs over the years and, although I love a beer or a good cider, I'm not so keen on spirits, not in shot form anyway. It's for that reason trying 'the world's hottest vodka' wasn't something I would ever have considered as a good idea, but in the end, we don't always have the luxury of choice.

When I was young and I first started going out drinking I found spirits very hard to deal with, a shot of vodka, an ordinary one, never mind the world's hottest, would leave me fighting not to bring it straight back up. It's only through years of practice that now, for the most part, I can hold my spirits without an issue and the times I've struggled… well I might as well tell you the best, or worst, of those too.

The earliest story I can recall where things went spectacularly wrong after drinking shots took place in around 1997, at a local Ipswich nightclub which was then called Hollywoods. Hollywoods was the place to go on a Monday for their rock night but after several name changes, and an incident where somebody was shot and killed in the club, it's now been turned into offices. Back in the day though, I was there every Monday without fail, and this particular night I'd gone with my friend Calvin and my girlfriend at the time, Rachel. The night had been going well but, after a round of cheap shots at the bar, I'd come over feeling the worse for wear. I left my friends and walked over to an area on the right of the dancefloor where people often left their coats and bags, I slumped down on top of them feeling very sick indeed. It was all I could do to sit there, it was taking all of my concentration just to do that and simultaneously hold the contents of my stomach where they should be, on the inside. The partially digested food in my stomach had other ideas though and it began to rebel against me like an acne ridden teen rising up against an overbearing parent, "Let me out," it screamed at me, "for God's sake, you never let me do what I want." I just needed to be left alone until the feeling passed, I strengthened my resolve and began to ride the wave. It didn't take long for Rachel to come and check on me, she was very concerned when she saw me sat alone in a corner and, being the nice girl, she was, she wanted to know if she could help in any way.

"Just don't touch me and I'll be alright." I told her bluntly. I felt very strongly that any sort of physical contact from anyone or anything would be enough to trigger an unwanted reaction, I needed time to diffuse the situation, just a minute or two more and everything would be under control.

Rachel lent down towards me, "I can help," she insisted, "maybe if you get up, you'll feel better." and, ignoring the one thing I'd asked her not to do, she took hold of my hands and tried to help me to my feet.

"Don't touch me!" I repeated as urgently as I was able, but it was too late, my young girlfriend was already yanking on my arms and, in doing so, caused a reaction that, for her, had both a positive and a negative outcome. Although in her eyes the positive, that her goal of making me feel better had been achieved, may have been a little hard to focus on after the negative happened.

Rachel's short, sharp tug on my arms had been enough, my body went into full expulsion mode and there was nothing I could do to halt the process. I opened my mouth like an erupting volcano and drenched my girlfriend in the most putrid of pukes, she froze, bent at a ninety-degree angle at the waist, her hands lost their grip on mine and hung loosely above the floor. She looked like a deactivated robot… covered in sick. I felt better, much better, I breathed a sigh of relief as I wiped my mouth with the back of my sleeve and clambered to my feet.

"I did tell you not to touch me." I told her, she remained motionless, as if waiting to reboot. Moments later the DJ played 'Hitchin' a Ride' by Green Day, in an instant, Rachel was forgotten, "Oh, I love this song!" I cried excitedly, turning my full attention back to the dancefloor and, as I disappeared into the crowd, I was pleased to feel a little lighter and a lot less bloated than I had been previously.

2010 was the year I got married to Jadie but, before that momentous occasion could occur, I had to endure one other formality, a traditional rite of passage and the path that all condemned men must walk, the stag night, or in my case, the stag weekend. My best man, Jason, had organised everything, we were going to Edinburgh, with our friends Calvin and Tom, to go canyoning, white water rafting and, it probably goes without saying, drinking. What a trip that was, there were so many good memories made that weekend. My personal highlight was the canyoning, jumping off rocks and cliffs into ice cold water is the best hangover cure I've ever known, and the white water rafting, while not as much fun as the canyoning it provided more laughs simply because I was given a wetsuit that was a least a full size too small for me. I looked like I'd been vacuum sealed.

On the second night we were in a pub, when Jason returned from the bar with a round of Jägerbombs, Jäger has never sat well with me and even today I'd be apprehensive about drinking a bomb, on this particular occasion my fears were well founded. Along with my cohorts I raised my glass and devoured the contents, no sooner had the last drop been swallowed I knew it wanted to come back, my eyes watered as I surveyed the faces of my friends, hoping against hope that I could regain control of this reflex. Jason caught my eye, we went back a long way and he'd seen the expression on my face before, he knew the telltale signs, "Keep it down mate." he begged, I frantically began to look around for somewhere, anywhere, to be sick. We were sat in a booth, the same kind you might find in a fifties diner, ours happened to be in the corner almost against the wall, they hadn't been able to fit it flush to the wall because the gap accommodated a radiator. The gap was only a little more than ten centimetres but it was enough, I leaned over and, being as subtle as I could, I proceeded to fill that gap. The smell in our booth, following my regurgitation, was not pleasant, and we quickly decided it would be best to move seats. It was interesting to watch the next group of people who sat there as they ate their meal, sniffing the air once in a while as they did so, never quite knowing where exactly the strange smell bothering them was coming from, while right next to them my vomit slowly evaporated into the air via the heat of the radiator.

One of my favourite bands is a two-piece punk rock outfit called Slaves, like The Wildhearts, Slaves are a band I've been to see all over the place and on this particular occasion I was travelling to London to watch them with Jason. On the way there, we stopped off at a little pub and decided to wet the whistle with a few beers and a couple of cheeky black sambucas. Of all the spirits sambuca was the one I probably found the easiest to stomach and so I was confident in my ability to drink as many of them as the situation required. The first shot went down easily enough and I moved on to the second which, regrettably, contained a hidden ingredient. As soon as I swallowed the tainted concoction, I knew I was in trouble, hidden within the dark liquor was a single hair, a hair that had mercilessly lodged itself at the back of my throat. This mystery hair's origin remains unknown but, best case scenario, it was one of my own beard hairs, worst case, it belonged to a member of staff in the bar. Of course, I fixated on the worst case and it was the combination of the feeling of the hair tickling the back of my throat, and the disgusting notion that it belonged to some unknown perpetrator, that proved to be my undoing that day. I gagged violently on the hair, suddenly my mouth was full of sick, gritting my teeth I performed a hard swallow forcing it back down again but it was no use, no sooner was it down than it came right back up again. Jason was sat next to me blocking my path to the bathroom, hastily I gestured for him to clear the way as I barged past him and sprinted, hand over mouth, to the bathroom. By the time I opened the bathroom door my mouth was full to bursting, I convulsed as I tried to hold it in and breathe at the same time, it was an impossible task but thankfully, at least, the bathroom was empty. Unable to wait any longer I opened my mouth and let rip, I couldn't help it, I couldn't even make it to the toilet, and I didn't much care considering I had, what I was sure was someone else's hair, in my throat. I was sick everywhere and I do mean everywhere. The toilet, the urinal, the sink, the floor, everywhere. Even when I thought I was done and made it back to my seat, it was mere seconds before I needed to run back and continue the expulsion. I threw up way beyond the point anyone would have considered themselves to be empty, to the point I wondered what else could possibly come out of me. After following me into the bathroom to pee, Jason took one look at the state of the area and we decided it might be best that we leave. We finished our drinks and moved on to a shop where, in order to dislodge the hair, I bought and ate a packet of twelve chocolate mini rolls. It did not work, and I felt ill for some time after.

    I'm glad I'm better these days at holding my drink, that's not to say I'm never sick anymore, it happens to the best of us, but it definitely happens a lot less than it used to and although shots are easier to drink than when I was younger that is not a rule that applies to every shot. One of our local bars, Yates, had started serving a chili vodka shot that was supposed to be one thousand one hundred times hotter than jalapeño peppers, I like spicy food but after hearing some horror stories about how bad this shot was, I had no intention of trying it myself. Another thing the bar served were paddles of flavoured shots, these were something I wasn't than keen on either as some of the flavours sounded revolting but at least the chili one wasn't included in the selection. Jason had gone to the bar and come back with one of these paddles of six shots, three each. We divided them up not entirely sure of the flavours we were getting but we both had one similar looking shot each that we saved for last as it seemed to be both colourless and odourless, therefore probably the safest of the three. Two shots down, we picked up the third and drank them down simultaneously. For a second I felt safe, it seemed like any other shot until suddenly, it didn't... Once the burn kicked in it was too late, with every second that passed my mouth got hotter, my throat was on fire and my lips were smoldering, not in a good way. It felt as though someone had declared my mouth dead, skipped the funeral and gone straight to the cremation, it was not a pleasant sensation. I looked over at Jason who was also not looking well, his eyes were streaming down his red face as he feebly croaked, "I've done one of those chili ones."

"Me too." I said forcing the words out of my throat, "I need some air." with purpose I got up from my seat and swiftly made my way to the exit, the heat was still building which, to be honest, was quite impressive, even when I thought hotter was impossible this vodka turned up the heat. I was ninety percent sure I was going to have to be sick and as I paced up and down outside the pub I looked back through the window at Jason who did not look like he was holding up well, with his eyes closed and his fists clenched he looked as though he was sitting in an electric chair. Managing, for once, to resist the urge to vomit, I headed back inside to rejoin my friend. Without a word, I sat down and took a sip of my strawberry and lime Kopparberg, I was so glad that had been the drink I'd chosen before the shots arrived because holding it my mouth gave me some much needed relief from the jalapeño burn, it was so refreshing I cannot even describe the feeling but as soon as I swallowed the liquid down the burn instantly returned with a vengeance. With minimal sips left of my beverage, and no way I could manage ordering another with a scorched throat, I sat there holding the cider in my mouth and did my best to get every moment relief I could out of what I had left.

To this day that vodka remains the hottest thing I have ever consumed, it didn't take long for the bar to stop serving it as unprepared customers were not handling it too well. A few months ago, however, Jason returned from the bar with another round of those shots, although they were not technically allowed to serve it anymore, the bottle had never been disposed of and had been sitting there waiting for us. I was understandably apprehensive but, once again, I took my medicine. Stupid!

These days, the culprit for a messy night out can usually be traced back to the playing of a game that Jason and I invented one evening called *The Age Game*. The rules of *The Age Game* are simple, but don't let that fool you into thinking surviving the game is so easy. The game is played thusly;

A player is chosen at random to go first, that person will select a celebrity.

> The remaining players will guess the age of said celebrity with the player who chose the celebrity in play being the last person to make a guess. You cannot select an age that has already been guessed by another player.
>
> If you correctly guess the age, or are the closest guesser within one year of the correct answer then you're safe, everybody else drinks. If nobody is correct, nobody drinks.

Play resumes with the person to the left choosing a new celebrity.

This game is surprisingly addictive, so much so that I'm writing this still a little hungover from a game played only last night. Next time you're on a night out give it a try. You're welcome.

Best Day Ever

One of my favourite television programs of all time is a show called *Impractical Jokers*, in which four real life friends, Joe, Sal, Murr and Q, interact with members of the public while their fellow jokers tell them what they have to do and say in that situation, if they refuse to do what they're told then they lose and the loser of each episode gets punished. From the first time the show aired I was hooked and no matter how many times I see an episode repeated I still find it funny. That being the case, when they announced a UK tour stopping at the O2 in London I knew I had to get tickets.

Before we knew it, the day of the show had arrived. Jason and I left Ipswich early in order to make the most of the day, so shortly after eight in the morning we were already on the train with a beer in hand. Some people might argue that drinking that early in the day isn't the best idea, normally I'd agree but sometimes you have to make an exception. We arrived at Liverpool Street Station in good time and high spirits, looking up at the station roof, or lack thereof, brought back memories of my last visit to London, the time when I'd gotten myself lost, I shivered and wrapped my coat tighter around my body, never again.

Having plenty of time to spare we decided to walk around London rather than jumping on the tube, we didn't have vast distances to travel so this would save us a few pounds which we could then invest back into beers. We set off towards the first pub of the day while talking about the *Impractical Jokers* and continuing the search for Larry, something my favourite joker Joe Gatto does on the show once in a while where he'll look for a fictional person by the name of Larry by running all over the place screaming his name. We got a few odd looks. By the time we'd hit a few pubs and had a few more drinks, we found ourselves on the banks of the Thames, the cold brown waters looked uninviting but as I looked down into the murky depths, I came to a realisation, I really needed to pee. My full bladder was a problem because there didn't seem to be a toilet anywhere close enough to accommodate my needs, except for the river Thames itself, and that was pretty risky due to the amount of people both walking along the bank and out on the river in boats. It was an option, but I didn't really feel like being arrested for exposure so it was a last resort. We carried on walking for a few more minutes and with each passing second, for me, things got more desperate, I hadn't been for a pee all day and I'd had multiple beverages, if that much goes in then sooner or later something has to come out, it's nature, you can't fight nature and with that in mind it was time to turn to the last resort.

As luck would have it we'd arrived at an area where some thick stone steps led directly down into the water, if I walked down close to the water perhaps I would be hidden from the walkers along the banks and I could keep my back to the boats, it was almost the perfect crime, ah the Thames, natures toilet. With an unplanned bladder release imminent, I started down the steps towards the water however, in my haste to unload my waste liquid I had forgotten something important, something that happens to stone steps when combined with both water and cold weather, they get a little... slippery. I hurried downwards, tackling steps one, two and three with little to no difficulty, my left foot connected with step four, this step did not have the same level of traction as it's slightly higher counterparts. Before I knew what was happening, I was airborne, I was literally flying.

I didn't think of much in that split second, I was in the air but later it occurred to me that it was the fourth step that got me, the fourth step! I remembered years earlier in that salsa lesson, I'd challenged that class when they'd missed out the four in their counting of the beats, "Where's the four?" I'd screamed at them. I imagined they'd be pretty pleased if they could see me in that moment as I trod on the fourth step, "There's your four," they'd say, "enjoy it."

I was falling, hurtling downwards towards terra firma at an alarming speed, I only prayed I could hold my bladder in check as I landed. My elbow connected first, hitting the stone with a crack moments before my back slammed into the ninety degree pointed step knocking the wind out of me, I'm underselling this ever so slightly when I say it hurt but I'd like to sound brave about the pain at least given that nothing else about this story reflects positively on me as a functioning human being. I'd like to be able to say the ordeal was over with the landing, that was not so because the steps were still slippery and my momentum, built up in the fall, now served to carry me further down the steps towards the waiting waters below. I half turned and desperately clawed at the steps in a futile effort to achieve purchase, I did not want to enter the Thames, not in the slightest, and luckily, as fate would have it, I stopped a hair shy of being dunked like a digestive biscuit in a mug of hot tea. As I lay there, just above the water, I watched it lap lightly against the stone steps and it seemed I could almost hear the river laughing at me, as if it had fired a warning shot to all would be polluters looking to unzip their trousers and add to the already dirty enough Thames, then I realised the laughter was real. Jason stood at the top of the steps in hysterics and, unable to help myself, I began to laugh as well, even though I was in a fair amount of pain the hilarity of the situation was not lost me, however, laughing made it harder not to empty my bladder into my trousers. I still had a mission to accomplish.

Very carefully, I got to my feet using the wall as support, the ground was extremely slippery but this time I managed to maintain my balance. I reached down and fumbled with my flies, urgently trying to free my peen from my jeans before it released a hot stream of urine down my leg, the fall had been bad enough without adding pissy trousers to the mix. No sooner had I caught hold of my piece than I happened to glance up for the first time since landing, it was then that I realised my secluded little piddle platform wasn't so secluded after all, in fact I was pretty much in plain sight and clearly visible to the other pedestrians who walked along the bank towards me. It was too late, the Kraken had been released, what could I do? I had to pee. So, there I stood, exposed by the water, adding my DNA into the London rivers and waterways while I chuckled to myself like some sort of unhinged river assassin. Job done, I zipped up and, very gingerly, made my way back up the stairs to where Jason was still doubled up in laughter and, in typical Jason fashion, I discovered he'd managed to get part of the ordeal on camera. Thanks for the help mate. The incident had been so funny I honestly can't remember a single time in my life when I've laughed more, we were laughing for hours, we watched the video clip back so many times and it was always funny, to this day, even the mention of it is enough to make either of us laugh.

By the time we made it to the O2 we were starving, Jason had mentioned a buffet restaurant called Jimmy's which was supposedly very nice, and it was all you can eat as well, which was good for me as I can eat a lot. We found the place quickly enough and were shown to a table where we ordered some beer before making our way to the buffet to fill our plates. We made the most of the buffet's all you can eat policy, returning for three full plates of food, we were stuffed almost to the point of needing to be carried out. As we sat there waiting for our food to digest we looked around for a waiter so we could get the bill, the restaurant was rammed to capacity, when we left there was a queue out the door for a table and with that in mind, it occurred to us that if one were so inclined, this would be a pretty easy place to leave without paying. There were people walking about all over the restaurant, waiters and waitresses ran back and forth serving drinks whist customers walked around the buffet filling their plates, neither of us had attempted a dine & dash before but I liked our chances were we to attempt it. After discussing the idea for a few minutes, we laughed it off and changed the subject to something less criminal and we resumed the search for someone to get us the bill.

It didn't take long before I was sick to death of waiting around, "Wait here mate I'm just going to grab a bit more dessert." I told Jason as I stood up from the table, plate in hand.

"You're getting more food, Jesus!" he replied in disbelief, "I couldn't eat another thing."

I left the table and walked up to the crowded buffet, there I nonchalantly placed my plate on a random counter and casually walked out like I was James Bond. Once outside I executed phase two of my plan, the restaurant was a floor up so I positioned myself behind where I estimated Jason was seated before taking out my phone and calling him.

"Hello." Jason sounded bewildered by my call but he was playing it cool, I knew from his single word response we were on the same page, down to business.

"Alright mate." I answered cheerfully doubling up the word count from his greeting, was it code, a one followed up by a two, it could have been, if I didn't know how would the law.

"Yeah, what are you doing calling me?" I could almost feel Jason looking across the restaurant wondering why it was his friend was calling him from the buffet, maybe there was some sort of new shrimp we'd missed the first time around that I just had to tell him about before returning to the table, maybe I wanted to know if I should bring him a nice slice of cake. We weren't on the same page after all, suddenly I felt less like James Bond and a little more like Johnny English.

I adopted a hushed tone, covert, you might say, "Look behind you." I whispered. There was a pause, a floor above Jason turned to look over his shoulder.

"There's nothing behind me." His tone was very matter of fact.

"Further." I replied, trying to get him to move off his seat.

"What do you mean further?" forget Johnny English, by this point we were barely Inspector Clouseau.

"Further." I repeated in the hopes he would understand what I was alluding to, "Look out the window."

"I am looking out the window." at last, a small victory, I looked up towards where I expected him to be, hoping to catch his eye but I couldn't see him anywhere.

I responded impatiently, "Well can you see me?"

Jason also sounded slightly annoyed by my cryptic instructions, "No of course not, you're at the buffet"

I was exasperated, "I'm not at the buffet, I'm outside, I think you're looking through the wrong window."

For a second Jason paused, "You left? Hold on." with that he hung up and, less than sixty seconds later, he joined me outside. We quickly decided from there the best thing to do was run, just in case we were noticed, and so we legged it through the O2 as fast as our recently stuffed bellies would allow.

Still with a few hours to kill before the *Impractical Jokers* we discussed what we should do next, now we were fugitives at large inside the O2. Of course, it was imperative that we keep a low profile and stay on high alert for any sign that we may have been followed or recognised from a description that had surely been handed out to every police officer in London. The trouble was, all that food had made us sleepy, it's hard to stay alert after eating three full plates of food, we needed a power nap but since we weren't staying overnight, we had nowhere safe to go to accomplish that. It was then that I had a moment of genius, we both had Cineworld membership cards and there was a Cineworld in the O2, we could go there to sleep and it would cost us nothing. So that's what we did, we booked the next film showing, which was the latest *Star Wars* movie, we took our seats and set our alarms for when we had to leave. I had never really enjoyed the *Star Wars* films, in fact they always seemed to put me to sleep, a lucky coincidence perhaps but it definitely helped me out that day. Even though I had absolutely zero interest in the film I do realise it was a popular movie so two sleeping guys, possibly snoring a bit I'm not sure, who had set an alarm to wake them part way through the film, would probably not be the most popular of movie-goers, but for us it was perfect as we were able to both hide from anyone who might be looking for us from Jimmy's buffet, and rest up for *Impractical Jokers* at the same time.

The show itself was fantastic and the perfect finish to a pretty flawless day, sure I was in a moderate amount of pain from the fall but it was one hundred percent worth it for sheer comedy value, if only every day could be so much fun.

Bowel Cancer

Firstly, don't be put off by that title, I don't have bowel cancer… not that I know of anyway, fingers crossed there. Nor is this the story of anyone I know with that condition, something else I'm grateful for. This story, like so many of my others, is a drinking story and it begins in Christchurch Park on April Fool's Day.

I was meeting up with Jason and our mutual friend Matt. Matt is someone I don't get to see that often as he doesn't live in Ipswich but the occasions when I do see him are always memorable. Memorable is a good word, unpredictable is another, Matt is a catalyst for carnage. I'll never forget the time we were all in our local Wetherspoons pub 'The Cricketers', when Matt returned from the bathroom brandishing several rolls of toilet paper. We were sat outside on a cold night and he'd decided to make a small bonfire on the table in order to keep us warm. It didn't take long for a member of staff to come outside to investigate the blazing table and eject us all from the pub, I'd seen this coming and swiftly began to down my drink, Jason clocked this and joined me as Matt argued with the barman that the blaze was under control, insisting there was nothing for him to be concerned about, as if four guys sat around an unauthorized bonfire was perfectly reasonable in a Wetherspoons beer garden.

Anyway, it was April Fool's Day, Jason and myself had met up with Matt in Ipswich town centre and we headed straight for the closest shop in order to procure some alcoholic refreshments before making the short walk over to Christchurch Park. When we arrived, we found a quiet bench to sit on and set about making short work of our selected beverages. Being April, it wasn't the hottest day but it was nice enough to drink outside and not be too cold, I enjoyed the warmth of the afternoon sun on my face as I drank my pineapple and raspberry cider. It certainly was a lovely day to be unemployed and drinking in a public park, suddenly, and I'm not sure entirely why, but I found myself feeling grateful that I had a home to go to.

As anyone who likes to binge drink will tell you, the alcohol is great but the amount of times you'll have to visit the little boys' room once you break the seal is nothing more than a pain in the arse. I may have mentioned earlier that I'm not a fan of public bathrooms, I do imagine the grass is greener on the other side though, the other side being the ladies' room. I imagine females, for the most part, would take care to leave a toilet in the same condition they found it, not like the men's cubicles where everything, including the floor, will probably be sprinkled with urine and /or fecal matter and you get hit with the smell of stale pee as soon as you enter, nope the ladies probably smells like the ocean, or flowers, or something else refreshing. On the few occasions I have entered, and used, a ladies' bathroom I remember it being clean at the very least. Men are definitely the losers when it comes to public bathrooms.

The public toilets in Christchurch Park are located to the right side of the park by the side entrance, well the cleanest ones are, there are alternatives but I wouldn't want to use them. We'd been going back and forth to these toilets, individually, for a few hours but this was the first time we all needed to use the facilities at the same time. Jason, who had entered first, quickly ducked into a cubicle locking the door behind him, these toilets were unusually pretty clean for a gents' so the cubicle was a good choice and, had I entered first, I'd have gone the same way. I surveyed the rest of the room and, although it appeared there was a second cubicle, I figured since the urinals were all free, I'd try my luck over there. I walked with purpose over to the urinal noticing, as I did so, the tangy, unpleasant smell that hung in the air and I wrinkled my face in revulsion. I unzipped my flies and had just established my stream when I heard the unmistakable sound of a loud fart echoing from out of the cubicle. Now this fart sounded very wet and very worrying, I raised an eyebrow and carried on pissing looking like Dwayne Johnson… and yes, I could smell what he was cooking. If it had been anyone else in the bathroom stepping on a duck, I'd have let it go and made a hasty retreat, but because it was Jason crop dusting the hell out of the place, I couldn't let it pass by without comment. I knew Jason would have had something to say about it if I'd been the one in there with King Kong's finger tickling my backside.

"What the hell was that?" I asked loudly, turning my head towards the cubicle door as I peed, expecting some sort of response, a sarcastic remark maybe or a quick one liner. Nothing, not a word, not even a Paul Blart. I turned my attention back to the task at hand and continued to rain on the bowl.

All finished I zipped up and moved to the sink just as Matt came breezing into the bathroom, he stood at the entrance and inhaled before loudly proclaiming, "Jesus Christ, it smells like bowel cancer in here." I laughed as I washed my hands while Matt walked to the urinal still sniffing the air like a nervous dog. As I went to leave the bathroom the cubicle door opened and Jason shot past me and out of the bathroom like a rocket. I followed him as he burst into laughter.

"What's wrong with you?" I asked slightly confused at what it was exactly that he found so amusing.

Jason was trying to stop laughing long enough to speak, he wasn't finding it easy. "There's... someone... else... in... there..." the tears streamed from his eyes as he struggled to catch his breath.

"You what? You mean...?" I looked back towards the bathroom.

"There's some guy in there having a shit... and every time he squeezed a bit out... either you or Matt commented on it." It hadn't even occurred to me that the other cubicle was occupied, and the realisation that I'd been loudly commenting on some stranger's bowel movements had me laughing just as much as Jason. When Matt reappeared both Jason and myself were still struggling to pull ourselves together, I hadn't laughed so hard since I nearly fell in the Thames. We left the park and retired to The Woolpack for another pint.

There have been many occasions I'm sure when we've all been caught short and had to avail ourselves of the nearest available public facilities. It could be worse though, what if there are no toilets close enough. I'll never forget the day after my eighteenth or nineteenth birthday, I was severely hungover and walking about five minutes away from Christchurch Park. I was at defcon one, condition critical, I had to find somewhere before the time of release became something that was no longer my choice. Next to me I noticed an open garage, inside was a shiny car mid wash, a bucket and sponge sat beside it but the owner was nowhere to be seen, presumably he'd slipped off to make a cup of tea or use the toilet himself. I had no choice, I'm not proud of this but I ran into the garage, pulled down my trousers and dropped the steaming hot deuce right next to the driver's side door. I cleaned myself up at lightning speed with some tissues I had in my jacket pocket which, as no alternative was available for disposal, I tossed under the car and then as fast as I could, I pulled up my trousers and ran for the hills. I thought for a long time about what that man saw when he returned to finish cleaning his car, he'd left the garage door open and unattended for only a few small minutes and now… well, he had to somehow remove my power dump from the concrete floor next to his pride and joy. I hope he had a jet wash.

The moral of this story I suppose, if you're the kind of person that craves a moral, would be to always go for your number two in the morning. Maintain a high fibre diet and leave on empty, that way, barring illness, you won't have to go in a stranger's garage or leave the public bathroom worrying that your excretion smells like you have a terminal illness.

Don't leave the house holding on to yesterday.

I did one just outside the front door to a church once as well, I was poorly at the time. Sorry.

Bonjour

When I was five years old, I chased a peacock. I ran after it without a second thought to my own safety or anything beyond my single-minded urge to catch that bird. I didn't even know what I wanted to do with it when I caught it. Maybe I've been chasing that bloody peacock my entire life, or at least a metaphorical version of it anyway. I suppose the only problem with a life spent chasing peacocks is that peacocks… well, peacocks are flipping fast.

Now I'm in my forties, I'd like to be able to say that I've reached that mythical place I talked about at the start of this book. That somehow in writing these words I have achieved a new understanding of my journey through life and become that normal, responsible, functioning human that, when I was a child, I thought all adults were and that I would have blossomed into a long time ago. I haven't. But maybe, in my daughter's eyes that's exactly who I am. Maybe the love, support and encouragement I give to them makes me that person in their lives. Maybe, without knowing it, I've already been the adult I thought I'd never be. We show our children the best of ourselves in the hope that they will grow up and not make the mistakes we made but, in the end, we're all going to get things wrong, that's life. The important thing is to be able to look back and embrace the good things and the bad, to cringe when you think about how you peed in a doctor's face but laugh with a fondness as warm as the urine that hit him at the same time. It's a good thing to look back on your life and be able to remember all the times you got it wrong, because that means you tried, it means you lived and it means you're human.

Or is that just bullshit?

Manufactured by Amazon.ca
Bolton, ON

12466051R00146